MUTED VOICE

MUTED VOICE

A Challenge to the Body of Christ to Speak Out Against Racism

Mike Moore

MIKE MOORE
MINISTRIES

DEDICATION

This book is dedicated to . . .

The 2,000 known black victims of racial-terror lynchings during the Reconstruction era between 1865 and 1876 after the Emancipation Proclamation and the end of the Civil War in America.

The 4,400 known black victims of lynching from the end of the Reconstruction era in 1877 and 1950.

The Civil Rights martyrs: [1]The Rev. Dr. Martin Luther King, Jr. (April 4, 1968), Rev. George Lee (May 7, 1955), Lamar Smith (August 13, 1955), Emmett Louis Till (August 28, 1955), John Earl Reese (October 22, 1955), Willie Edwards, Jr. (1957), Mack Charles Parker (April 25, 1959), Herbert Lee (September 25, 1961), Cpl. Roman Ducksworth, Jr., (April 9, 1962), Paul Guihard (September 30, 1962), William Louis Moore (April 23, 1963), Medgar Evers (June 12, 1963), Addie Mae Collins, Denise McNair, Carole Robinson and Cynthia Wesley (Children killed in a church bomb-September 15, 1963), Virgil Lamar Ware (September 15, 1963), Louis Allen (January 31, 1964), Johnnie Mae Chappell (March 23, 1964), Rev. Bruce Klunder (April 7, 1964), Henry Hezekiah Dee and Charles Eddie Moore (May 2, 1964), James Earl Chaney, Andrew Goodman and Michael Henry Schwerner (June 21, 1964), Lt. Col. Lemuel Penn (July 11, 1964), Jimmie Lee Jackson (February 26, 1965), Rev. James Reeb (March 11, 1965), Viola Greg Luizzo (March 25, 1965), Deputy Oneal Moore (June 2, 1965), Willie Brewster (July 18, 1965), Jonathan Myric Daniels (August 20, 1965), Samuel Leamon, Jr. (January 3, 1966), Vernon Ferdinand Dahmer (January 10,1966), Ben Chester White (June 10, 1966), Charlene Triggs (July 30, 1966), Wharlest Jackson (February 27,

---

1 https://www.splcenter.org/what-we-do/civil-rights-memorial/civil-rights-martyrs

1967), Benjamin Brown (May 12, 1967), Samuel Ephesians Hammond Jr., Delano Herman Middleton and Henry Ezekial Smith (February 8, 1968).

All the unarmed black people killed by police since the late 1960s including the over 300 unarmed black people killed by police from 2013-2019 and the 164 black people killed by police in the first eight months of 2020.

The countless thousands of black victims murdered in America, a land dedicated to the premise that God created all of us equal.

CONTENTS

These six things doth the Lord hate: yea, seven are an
abomination unto him:
*A proud look, a lying tongue, and **hands that shed innocent blood**,*
An heart that deviseth wicked imaginations,
feet that be swift in running to mischief,
A false witness that speaketh lies,
and he that soweth discord among brethren.

Proverbs 6:16-19 KJV

Introduction
A Muted Voice Is No Voice

"The ultimate tragedy is not the oppression and cruelty by bad people,
but the silence over that by good people." [2]
—Martin Luther King, Jr.

On June 19, 2020, I received a prophetic word from the Holy Spirit. He said to me, "a muted voice is no voice." The word *mute* means silent voice, refraining from speech, not uttering something that is thought and felt. Sometimes, while my wife and I are watching television, she will ask me to mute the television. When I do so, the television goes silent; then, we can talk. After our dialogue, I unmute the sound and continue to watch and hear what's being broadcasted.

Let me unpack this for you briefly. When Nehemiah was rebuilding the walls of Jerusalem, his workers did not have time to raise animals to feed their families. The Jews not working on the wall and living outside the city grew crops and raised flocks of sheep and goats to sell food to the wall builders. But food was expensive, and Nehemiah's workers

2 https://www.brainyquote.com/quotes/martin_luther_king_jr_390143

could not afford the food, so they began mortgaging their homes and selling their children as slaves in exchange for food. Socio-economic racism was happening among the Jews and when Nehemiah confronted this evil, we read, "They were silent [kept quiet, mute, dumb: Heb. OT:2790 vr^j* *charash*]; because they could find nothing to say." Nehemiah confronted the socio-economic racism within the Jewish people of his day. They had kept silent about the injustice. There was no excuse for their racist actions and attitudes.

Likewise, in America today, the Church—the whole Body of Christ (Protestant, Catholic, and Orthodox) within much of its leadership, has been *charash*, [had a muted voice] about racism within both Church and Culture. The passage of the Civil Rights legislation in the 1960s has not eliminated the poverty, social and legislative injustices, or the enslavement of scores of people of color [Black, Hispanic, Asian, Native American and many other minorities] in low-paying jobs or urban ghettos filled with violence, drugs, crime and murders.

The American Church's voice
has been muted about racism.

As a Christian leader, I feel called by God to challenge the Body of Christ to speak out against racism. Following the murder of George Floyd on May 25, 2020, mass protests in all fifty U.S. states and the District of Columbia have turned into a global movement for racial equality. An unusual awareness of racial injustice has created a desire for reformation across large spectrums of society. There is a desire for reformation in government, in education, in the military, in the business world, in the entertainment world, and in the sports world. Many institutions in our present day are speaking out against racism.

Some are even discussing laws, policies, and practices that need to be changed. Businesses are changing the names of racially offensive products and advertisements, while others are giving large donations to universities and other organizations toward reformation and racial equality. However, when we look at the Church, the Body of Christ's response, we see and hear silence, *charash*, . . . our voice is muted.

In a virtual meeting with our staff, the leader of the meeting was introducing the meeting purpose which was for me to cast the vision about the upcoming Muted Voice series. While they talked, I muted myself. I could hear and see the other teammates. Then, when it was my time to talk, I started talking but they couldn't hear me. They said, "Pastor, you are muted." I had to UNMUTE myself so that they could hear me. All of us in the Body of Christ, must unmute ourselves on this systemic issue of racism that has persisted since the arrival of the first enslaved Africans in Jamestown in 1619. Racism is a systemic sin.

I am convinced beyond a shadow of a doubt that when it comes to racism, even though the world has started to make changes toward equality, the Church of the Lord Jesus Christ has a muted voice.

First they came for the socialists, and I did not speak out—
because I was not a socialist.
Then they came for the trade unionists, and I did not speak out—
because I was not a trade unionist.
Then they came for the Jews, and I did not speak out—
because I was not a Jew.
Then they came for me—
and there was no one left to speak for me.
—Pastor Martin Niemöller [3]

---

[3] "Martin Niemöller (1892–1984) was a prominent Lutheran pastor in Germany. He emerged as an outspoken public foe of Adolf Hitler and spent the last seven years of Nazi rule in concentration camps."
https://encyclopedia.ushmm.org/content/en/article/martin-niemoeller-first-they-came-for-the-socialists

Niemöller [4], Dietrich Bonhoeffer, a Lutheran pastor, theologian, anti-Nazi dissident, along with many other evangelical believers in the era of Nazi Germany believed that Germans were **complicit through their silence** about the Nazi imprisonment, persecution, and murder of millions of people. They felt this was particularly true of German Christian leaders in the church. We are facing such a time as this again in the Church.

The original intent of the Gospel is to publish Good News to all people, at all times, and in all situations. The denouncement of all forms of discrimination, disease, and enslavement of body, soul and spirit is proclaimed by the unmuted voice of Christ:

"The Spirit of the Lord is upon Me,
Because He has anointed Me
To preach the gospel to the poor;
He has sent Me to heal the brokenhearted,
To proclaim liberty to the captives
[AMP: downtrodden, bruised, crushed, and broken down by calamity]
And recovery of sight to the blind,
To set at liberty those who are oppressed;
[NLT: the oppressed will be set free]
To proclaim the acceptable year of the Lord."
(Luke 4:18-19)

Knowing the truth of Christ in the Gospel, sets us free to proclaim, live, and if necessary, die for the Truth. Have you been silent in the face of wrongdoing? Have you been muted about racism?

A MUTED VOICE IS NO VOICE!

---

4 https://encyclopedia.ushmm.org/content/en/article/martin-niemoeller-first-they-came-for-the-socialists

Chapter 1
What Is Racism

"Silence in the face of evil is itself evil.
God will not hold us guiltless.
Not to speak is to speak, not to act is to act."[5]
—**Dietrich Bonhoeffer**, a Lutheran pastor martyred
in the Holocaust

As we begin this study on racism, I want to first talk about the off-spring of racism: prejudice, hatred, and discrimination. [6] Often, when we talk about racism, you hear these three words. So that you and I have the same definition and denotation about these words, let me provide you with a glossary for how I am using these terms in this book.

Prejudice. The word prejudice means to prejudge . . . embracing a preconceived negative opinion that is not based on authentic, personal knowledge or experience. Prejudice arises from hearsay, stereotypes,

5 www.goodreads.com/author/quotes/29333.Dietrich_Bonhoeffer

6 Adapted from Robin Diangelo, "White Fragility"

and generalizations. When we talk about prejudice, it has to do with our THOUGHTS which lead us to speak words that defame, degrade, and demean others . . .

"Dr. Gordon Allport, a social psychology professor and author, describes in his book, 'The Nature of Prejudice,' a five-stage process of how the utterance of slurs and hateful labels become weapons of dehumanizing a specific group of persons. The social soil of heightened prejudice now becomes cultivated in this [1] early phase of having these targeted persons to be perceived more as objects.

Thus, sct in motion is an incubating momentum for the next four phases of a gradual lethal process to evolve. These overlapping stages become [2] social avoidance, [3] discrimination (both social and often legal), [4] physical attack and [5] extermination. [7]

Hatred. On the other hand, hatred can be a deeply negative emotion or hostility felt towards certain races. Most people say, "I don't have hatred in my heart." But hatred can be a little more subtle than that. Hatred can also be the discomfort and the uneasiness that we have around certain racial groups that prompt us to want to segregate ourselves or to draw away from others. In other words, "I don't hate them, but I don't like to be around those people. In fact, I believe you should just stay with your own kind." When we talk about hatred, it has to do with our EMOTIONS. Prejudice has to do with our thoughts.

Discrimination. Discrimination is the natural response based on our prejudice. Discrimination would involve ignoring other races, exclusion, and withdrawing. It would include threats, ridicule, slander, or violence. Discrimination has to do with our ACTIONS.

REFLECTION STEPS

How has learning about these three offspring of racism impacted your understanding of racism?

---

7 https://www.thestate.com/opinion/letters-to-the-editor/article233992197.html

- Prejudice has to do with our thoughts.
- Hatred has to do with our feelings and emotions.
- Discrimination has to do with our actions.

What Is Racism?

I came up with two basic definitions of racism which really have to do with two schools of thought:

1. *Racism is the belief that race and skin color account for differences in human character, intelligence, ability, beauty, or civility that results in partiality toward one race and prejudice against another.* In other words, racism is attributing different qualities, whether they are negative qualities or positive qualities, to different racial groups. This means racism is the belief that one race is innately superior to another. So, if one race is superior, that means another race is inferior. It is applying positive qualities to the perceived superior race and applying negative qualities to the perceived inferior race. Evidence of this is when we think of one race and we say, "They are this way," and attach a quality that we believe constitutes superiority. Then we think of the other race and say, "They are this way" and attach a quality we believe is inferior. This is racism.

2. The second definition of racism is, *"Racism is a power relationship or struggle between groups of people who are competing for resources and political power."* [8] For example, in 2016, former San Francisco Forty-Niners quarterback, Colin Kaepernick, decided to kneel during the national anthem at an NFL game to protest racial injustice and police brutality.

President Donald Trump changed the narrative to describing it as dishonoring our country and the military. Vice President Mike Pence

---

8 www.goodreads.com/author/show/21938.Claud_Anderson

followed suit by going to an NFL game where he knew the players would be kneeling and he counter-protested by walking out before the game was played. Thirty-two NFL owners submitted to the pressure. The NFL banned kneeling during the anthem. Kaepernick, for all practical purposes, was released and apparently banned from playing in the NFL.

I must pause here. Racism often hides under the guise of patriotic nationalism. As we saw with Nazi Germany, patriotism was defined with extreme nationalism that saw one nation and that nation's ethnic majority as being greater than and superior to other nations and ethnic groups. Here's a revealing summary of how patriotism gets amalgamated and distorted by extreme nationalism:

> [9]*Nationalism is one of the most dangerous forces in the modern world, playing a major role in the origin of both World War I and World War II. Nationalism is the belief that one's country is superior to others. President Trump's "America First" doctrine is clearly extreme nationalism, leading him to denigrate countries in Africa, Latin America and the Muslim world . . . .*
>
> *Racism, too, is a dangerous force in history. President Trump's racist language, tweets and his racist theater for the masses aims to castigate black people, Latinos and Muslims at home and abroad.*
>
> *It is clear that Trumpism is built on extreme nationalism and racism, destructive forces that make the world a more dangerous place, increases hatred and xenophobia.*

Extreme nationalism crucified Christ from a Roman mindset. Even though Jesus declared His kingdom was not of this world, Pilate and the Roman rulers clearly saw Jesus and the emerging group of Jesus followers as a threat to Roman superiority and rule. A universal, divine

---

9 https://www.thestate.com/opinion/letters-to-the-editor/article233992197.html

ruler like Christ and His followers must be exterminated if any king-dom of the world is to rule and control people. Extreme nationalism and racism, a deadly duo, will also lead to martyrdom and genocide.

The only mindset that can ultimately confront and overcome rac-ism is the mind of Christ.

Recently, the commissioner of the NFL, Roger Goodell, admitted that the NFL was wrong for not allowing players to peacefully protest. In other words, he admitted that they had made a mistake. Joe Lock-hart, a former NFL executive, acknowledged that Kap, referring to Colin Kaepernick, was bad for business.

Was the situation with Kaepernick, the commissioner, the NFL owners, and their decision a business situation, a mistake, or was it racism?

🔇

"Racism isn't a bad habit.
It is not a mistake.
Racism is a sin.
The answer is not in sociology,
it is in theology."[10]
—Tony Evans

🔇

Claud Anderson's definition was that *racism is a power relationship or a struggle between groups of people.* Could it be that this situation with the NFL was a power relationship? Could it be that this was a struggle between the NFL, the owners, and the players? Were they competing for resources and political power?

Political power is the ability to control the behavior of people and influence the outcome of events through the passage, approval, and im-plementation of laws and regulations. Did the NFL control the players' behavior and determine the outcome by the passage of regulations and

---

10 https://sermonquotes.com/authors/9746-racism-isnt-bad-habit.html.Tony_Evans

laws? Remember, they banned kneeling during the anthem.

When it comes to racism, we must stop calling racism just a mistake. I challenge the Church to call it what it is and realize we have racism in the Body.

🔇

Racism can occur at both an unconscious and conscious level and it can be both active and passive.

🔇

We all know it's possible to operate in racism at a conscious level. Oftentimes, we point to the white supremacist group and say, "Hey, I'm not like them. That's the white supremacist group. They are racists." They are actively engaged in racism.

However, racism can also occur at an unconscious level. You can engage in racism in a passive way. You can just be quiet. You can be silent, muting your voice like the Church today. Christians in America have been called The Silent Majority. We must unmute and speak the truth to all parts of our culture: government/military, the arts/entertainment, media, education, religion, business/finance, and family. Though there is the beginning of reformation and awareness of racism all around us, it is like we have a muted voice. A muted voice is passive racism. Racism is anti-equality.

🔇

Racism is against the biblical position of equality in Christ.

🔇

Acts 17:26 says, "And he hath made from one blood every nation of man to dwell on the face of the earth." Galatians 3:28 says, "In Christ's family there can be no division into Jew and non-Jew, slave and free, male and female, among us you are all equal" (MSG). If you're born again, if you are a Christian, then you are in Christ's family. That would include every race and color; we are all equal in Christ.

The Bible is God's Word to us. We are not to decide how we live. God has given us His revelation. The Bible reveals God's thoughts, how He feels, and His perspective. When we read the Bible, we see that God's heart is complete equality in the Body of Christ.

◀×

That means the Body of Christ is raceless.
The Church is raceless.

◀×

2 Corinthians 5:17 declares, "Therefore if any man be in Christ, he is a new creation, he's a new creature." That means the Body of Christ consists of a new species. The Church is a new creation, a new species. The Church is composed of divine ethnicity. We are a divine ethnicity. Now, here are the statements I want you to really grasp and understand.

◀×

Christianity fully embraced and fully lived out,
equals equality.
Racism fully embraced and fully lived out,
equals superiority and inferiority.

◀×

How did the Church's voice become muted?
We know that Satan works through lies. In fact, Jesus in John 8:44 said that the devil is the father of lies and calls him a murderer. Jesus connected Satan's ability to murder, steal, kill, and destroy with lies. *How did the Church become muted?* How in the world can everyone around us in the government, the sports world, the entertainment world, and all these other institutions be open to reformation and racial equality,

yet the Church have a muted voice? What was the lie that silenced the Church?

The lie that silenced the Church is the lie of the curse of Ham. This is so very important. All issues and problems have a root. I am convinced beyond a shadow of a doubt that the root of racism in America is this so-called curse of Ham. It is found in Genesis 9:18-27. Walk with me through these verses and I will reveal to you the misconceptions the Christian world has embraced and then explain the truth we need to implement in the Church today.

*[18] And the sons of Noah, that went forth of the ark, were **Shem, and Ham, and Japheth**: and **Ham is the father of Canaan**.*

[19] These are the three sons of Noah: and of them was the whole earth overspread.

[20] And Noah began to be an husbandman, and he planted a vineyard:

[21] And he drank of the wine, and was drunken; and he was uncovered within his tent.

*[22] And **Ham, the father of Canaan, saw the nakedness of his father**, and told his two brethren without.*

*[23] And Shem and Japheth took a garment, and laid it upon both their shoulders, and went backward, and covered the nakedness of their father; and their faces were backward, and **they saw not their father's nakedness**.*

*[24] And Noah awoke from his wine, and **knew what his younger son** had done unto him.*

*[25] And he said, **Cursed be Canaan**; a servant of servants shall he be unto his brethren.*

*[26] And he said, Blessed be the LORD God of **Shem**; and **Canaan shall be his servant.***

*[27] God shall enlarge **Japheth, and he shall dwell in the tents of Shem; and Canaan shall be his servant.*** (KJV emphasis added)

The text begins, "And the sons of Noah, that went forth of the ark, were Shem, and Ham, and Japheth and that Ham is the father of Canaan." **Note** two things from this verse.

1. First, the order the sons are listed seems to put Ham in the middle of the birth order. [11]
2. Secondly, it says Ham was the father of Canaan. Then in verse 22, it says again that Ham was the father of Canaan. Right away that tells us that Canaan is a major player in the text.

The Bible says that after the flood, Noah became a farmer and he planted a vineyard. Then in verse 21, we read that Noah got drunk from the wine. **Note** that this did not happen the next day. It takes years for the vines to produce grapes and then more time to make the grapes into a fermented wine. [12]

Then we are told Noah was "uncovered" in his tent, and Ham saw his father's nakedness. He went out, told his two brothers, Shem and Japheth, who grabbed a garment, put it on their shoulders and they walked backwards into the tent and covered their father's nakedness. It clearly says Shem and Japheth **did not** see the nakedness of their father. Then it says when Noah awoke from his drunkenness and knew what his **younger son** had done, **he cursed Canaan** and said **Canaan** would be a servant of Shem.

This text was a favorite text of southern preachers (in America) during the Civil War. There were three basic things that the preachers on the confederate side were preaching. They preached that God cursed Ham, who was the father of the black race, and He cursed Ham's descendants which would include all people of color. However, that was

---

11 Again in Genesis 10, the Bible seems to list Ham as the second son of Noah.

12 Making wine is a long, slow process. It can take a full three years to get from the initial planting of a brand-new grapevine through the first harvest, and the first vintage might not be bottled for another two years after that. https://learn.winecoolerdirect.com/life-cycle-of-a-wine-grape/

a **LIE**. They also said that black people were made inferior and subservient to whites. That was also a **LIE**. Finally, they concluded that the mark of the curse is the black color of their skin. That was another **LIE**.

ASK YOURSELF . . .

- What have you heard about the curse of Ham?
- Do you believe God put a curse on the descendants of Ham?
- Do you believe God cursed black people?
- Do you believe black people were made subservient to whites?
- Do you believe they were made inferior?
- Do you believe the curse on black people was the black color of the skin?

Truth #1. We do not read anywhere in this text that Ham was cursed by God. To come up with that conclusion, we would have to add something to the text. In fact, it says in Genesis 9:1, God blessed Noah and his sons. This did not exclude Ham.

Truth #2. The Bible does not say that Ham sinned. It says he saw the nakedness of his father. What does that mean? Does that mean he saw his father naked or does it mean he saw something else?

Truth #3. The curse was declared by Noah, not God.

In Genesis 9:24, it says when Noah woke up from his drunken stupor, he knew what had happened. He knew what **his younger son** had done. This could not be a reference to Ham because Ham was not Noah's youngest son. Ham was Noah's middle son. The Bible didn't say he cursed Ham. The Bible says he cursed Canaan. What did Ham have to do with it? The truth is the curse had nothing to do with the black race. There is nothing in the text that says God cursed the black race.

Genesis 10:6 reports that Ham had three other sons. Canaan wasn't Ham's only son and he is listed as the youngest son of Ham. Ham had a son named Cush, he had a son named Mizraim, and he had a son named Phut. There is no mention of a curse on Cush, there is no mention of a curse on Mizraim, and there is no mention of a curse on Phut. If the black race were cursed, then there would have to be a curse on those other three sons, but there is no curse because there was no curse placed on black people. The curse placed on Canaan and his descendants was not a perpetual curse. It was not an eternal curse. It was a curse that was fulfilled when Joshua and the children of Israel conquered the Canaanite nation in the land of promise.

What did Ham see?

We return to what Ham saw. Ham saw something. The Bible says in verse 22 that Ham saw the nakedness of his father. The word nakedness has multiple meanings in the Bible.

Nakedness: [def] nudity
Nakedness: [def] a shameful or disgraceful act
Nakedness: [def] sexual intercourse

What was it that Ham saw? Did he see nudity, did he see shameful and disgraceful acts, or did he see sexual intercourse? Remember, nakedness can refer to the nakedness of a man or a woman.

None of you shall approach to any that is near of kin to him, to uncover their nakedness: I am the LORD. The nakedness of thy father, or the nakedness of thy mother, shalt thou not uncover: she is thy mother; thou shalt not uncover her nakedness. The nakedness of thy father's wife shalt thou not uncover: it is thy father's nakedness. (Leviticus 18:6-8 KJV)

I have found something very interesting in Leviticus 18:6-8. In the Amplified Translation, verse 6 says, "No one shall approach any blood relative of his to uncover nakedness (have intimate relations). I am the LORD." The text says God instructs His people to not have sexual relations with kinfolk. Verse 8 says the nakedness of the wife is the nakedness of the husband.

So, what did Ham see? Did he see Noah's nakedness? That's what most people think. But why does it have to be Noah's nakedness? Why can't it be his wife's nakedness because the Bible says that a husband's wife is his nakedness? I am convinced that Ham saw and caught Canaan, his son, having sex with his grandmother, Noah's wife. It would become easier for you to get this if you think about the Canaanites and how they were driven out and why they were driven out. The people of Sodom and Gomorrah were descendants of Canaan. They were doing all kinds of sex: sex with children, with the same sex, and incest. Remember, Lot's daughters had sex with their daddy. Where did they get that idea from? They got it from living under the influence of Sodom and Gomorrah.

Why is this so very important? Dr. C.I. Scofield was an American theologian, minister, and writer who is considered by some to be the most influential man in evangelical history. His reference Bible, published in 1909, became the standard for a generation of fundamental Christians. In his personal notes, he states that Genesis 9:24-25 is a prophetic declaration that says from Ham will descend an inferior and servile posterity. That is what Scofield taught. Inferior means low in rank. Servile means a slave and menial positions in life.

The Scofield Reference Bible and Scofield gave status and popularity to the theory of the curse of Ham to generations of Christians and ministers throughout the evangelical world. Where did Scofield get his beliefs from? Most people don't know this, but Scofield served a short time in the Civil War on the side of the Confederate States of America. The Civil War was fought over the moral and economic issues of slavery. The southern preachers during that time were preaching about the curse of Ham.

In other words, I'm saying I believe that this curse of Ham is the root of American racism. I also believe that Scofield popularized it and got it out through generations of evangelicals. I think that it is a shame.

Jeremiah 16:19 says, "Surely our fathers have inherited lies" (KJV). This appears to be what happened concerning this so-called curse of Ham.

We can conclude that a muted voice is no voice. It is racist to be aware of a biased situation and permit it to exist. It is, in fact, passive racism. **SILENCE IS COMPLICIT.** Silence is a passive form of racism

God is challenging the Church, and the Body of Christ, to speak out against racism.

REFLECTION STEPS

Begin by reviewing the Scriptures presented in this chapter, specifically the ones listed below. Study them in the light of the questions confronting us as the Church and the Body of Christ. Record your insights.

Acts 17:26

Galatians 3:28

2 Corinthians 5:17

Then review these Power Points set apart in Chapter 1:
- "Racism isn't a bad habit. It is not a mistake. Racism is a sin. The answer is not in sociology, it is in theology." [13]
- Racism can occur at both an unconscious and conscious level and it can be both active and passive.
- Racism is against the biblical position of equality in Christ.
- That means the Body of Christ is raceless. The Church is raceless.
- Christianity fully embraced and fully lived out equals equality.
- Racism fully embraced and fully lived out equals superiority and inferiority.

---

13 www.goodreads.com/author/quotes/2411.Tony_Evans

Dare to Confront with the Truth & Act Justly

As you read through these Power Points, what did God "dare" you to do to begin to "unmute" the members of the Body of Christ that may be living under the influence of the lies perpetrated by Satan?

_____

_____

_____

Pray and ask God to show you the first steps He wants you to take with each of the people you have listed.

_____

_____

_____

Record in a journal the response you received. Continue praying for revelation for each of these people.

Chapter 2
Five Social Viruses of Racism

The Prevalence of Infection

> *In 1963, Dr. Martin Luther King Jr.'s rebuke was,*
> *"The most segregated hour of Christian America is*
> *eleven o'clock on Sunday morning."[14]*

The prevalence of infection in medical terms has to do with the percentage of individuals in a population infected with a given pathogen. A pathogen is an organism that causes disease. How widespread is racism in the Body of Christ? Fifty-seven years after Dr. Martin Luther King Jr.'s statement, the Church remains overwhelmingly racially divided. Ninety percent of African American Christians worship at all black churches. Ninety percent of white American Christians worship in all white churches. *You might ASK YOURSELF, what's wrong with that?*

---

14 http://www.godandculture.com/blog/sunday-at-11-the-most-segregated-hour-in-this-nation

**The white Church and the black Church are a perversion
of God's plan for His Body.
Racist division in the Church is an alteration
and a distortion of God's original intent.**

Racial division in the Body of Christ is a social construct. Racial separation is a human invented classification system that runs counter to 1 Corinthians 1:10 that says, "there be no division among you." The American segregated Church was founded on and birthed out of two racist concepts—segregationism and white supremacy. Segregationism is the belief that equality is impossible because of the innate superiority of the white race and the innate inferiority of the black race. White supremacy is a concept that identifies white people and white culture as normal and superior.

Remember that Original Sin arising from the Fall in Genesis is rooted in pride. Such pride declares, "I am God," and thus separates us from God and from others. It is the opposite of *loving others as we love ourselves.* God's original intent was for human beings, **all** of whom are created in His image, to live and dwell in His presence as one family united by selfless love. Racism separates and divides us just as prideful, original sin divided Adam and Eve from God while separating them and pitting them against one another. The ultimate consequence of racism that originated in the Fall is selfish, shameful pride.

**The racist, separated, prideful, sinful Church today
ought to be ashamed of itself!**

That they all may be one; as thou, Father, art in me, and I in thee, that they also may be one in us: that the world may believe that thou hast sent me.

And the glory which thou gavest me I have given them; that they may be one, even as we are one: I in them, and thou in me, that they may be made perfect in one; and that the world may know that thou hast sent me, and hast loved them, as thou hast loved me. (John 17:21-23 KJV)

I believe one of the greatest mortal sins in the Body of Christ and the greatest threat to God's plan of revival in the United States is racism. In John 17:21-23, Jesus prayed that His Body would be united, that His Body be one. Unity is essential for the Church to manifest God's glory and is also essential to our witness as the family of God being light to the world.

Psalm 133:1-3 says, "Behold, how good and how pleasant it is for brethren to dwell together in unity! It is like the precious ointment upon the head, that ran down upon the beard, even Aaron's beard: that went down to the skirts of his garments; As the dew of Hermon, and as the dew that descended upon the mountains of Zion: for there the LORD COMMANDED THE BLESSING, EVEN LIFE FOR EVERMORE" (KJV). This talks about how good and how pleasant it is for brethren to walk together and about the oil (the anointing) and the dew (productivity) all connected to oneness.

In John 17, Jesus connects this united body and oneness to His glory, His manifested presence, and our witness. God connects His anointing, His blessing, His glory, the believer's productivity and the Church's witness to oneness, to unity.

In Acts 13:1, we see the first Christian Church in Antioch was a multiracial, multicultural Church (see Acts 13:1).

Now there were in the church that was at Antioch certain prophets and teachers; as Barnabas, and Simeon that was called Niger, and Lucius of Cyrene, and Manaen, which had been brought up with Herod the tetrarch, and Saul. (KJV)

ASK YOURSELF . . .
- How does all this speak about unity in the Body of Christ's Church today?

Spiritual Illness in the Body of Christ

I believe the Church is spiritually ill and is in ICU, hooked up to respirators, comatose, and unable to speak. We are so incapacitated as the Body of Christ, that God has been forced to look outside of the Church to work. We are in a precarious position spiritually when we have a spiritual illness and we do not know it.

How did the Church get so sick?

There are five social viruses of racism:
- Generational Racism,
- Environmental Racism,
- Institutional Racism,
- Economic Racism, and
- Reactionary Racism.

Generational Racism. Jeremiah 16:19b says, "surely our fathers have inherited lies" (KJV). Generational Racism is when beliefs, attitudes, or false concepts of others are passed from one generation to the next generation through teaching, modeling, and experience. In the field of social science, generational racism is the byproduct and the result of negative racial socialization. Racial and Ethnic Socialization (RES) has to do with the direct and indirect explicit messages which children receive about race, racial groups, and their role in society.

22

All children are socialized and gain information about racial groups from parents, family members, teachers, clergy, coaches, media, TV, news, advertisements, and publications. For example, when a child looks at a magazine and his or her race is highly represented that is an indirect message. When a child looks at a pageant and his/her representation is low, that is an indirect implicit message.

Racial socialization can be intentional. For example, a black parent intentionally buys her daughter a black doll. This black parent also buys books for her children with black main characters. That's socialization. On the other hand, I was watching the news the other day and they showed a group of people protesting and there was a white family who had their little child walking in the protest holding up a sign, "Black Lives Matter." That is either intentional or unintentional racial socialization in a positive way.

I'm reminded of a story Steve Harvey told about when he was in the sixth grade. The teacher gave the students an assignment where they were to tell the teacher what they wanted to be when they grew up. Steve Harvey said he wanted to be on television. The teacher thought that was absurd and unrealistic; she notified his parents that little Steve had been a smart aleck in school that day. So, when Steve got home, his parents were talking about it and he thought he was going to get in trouble. His mother initially bought into what the teacher had said but his father asked, "Well, what's wrong with him wanting to be on television?" When his father sent Steve to his bedroom, he thought his daddy was going to punish him. However, his dad said, "Now, you write what you believe on a piece of paper, put it in your drawer. Every morning, you read that paper about you being on television and read it every night before you go to bed."

If the comments the teacher had made about Steve had not been interrupted by his father, then he would have been socialized to think that TV was too far beyond his ability and his capacity.

My daughter, Tiffany, is a beautiful, intelligent, smart young lady.

When she was about four or five, we sent her to a wonderful Christian school. Tiffany came home one day all excited because she had played with this little white girl in her class. We asked her what game they had played, and she said they played mama and maid. My first thought was who was the maid. She told us she was the maid. I'll be honest with you, I had to repent. I wasn't sweet at all. I looked Tiffany in the face and said, "You are never going to be anybody's maid." By that I meant that often maids in our culture are people of color, and we should not use that stereotype. Generational racism and the sense of superiority and inferiority are both conditioned by our society.

**Generational racism is really the result of
negative racial ethnic socialization.**

Environmental Racism. In the first century A.D., Jews had no dealings or association with the Gentiles. In fact, the Jews in the New Testament days believed they were a superior race and the Gentiles were inferior. Therefore, no Orthodox Jew would ever cohabitate, engage, or associate with Gentiles. Then the Spirit of God spoke to Peter and told him to go to a Gentile's house and share the gospel (see Acts 10). He obeyed and there was a great outpouring of the Spirit, but when he came back to Jerusalem, his Jewish brethren reprimanded him. In Acts 11:3, they said to Peter, "You went into the homes of people who are not circumcised and you ate with them" (NCV).

This is an example of environmental racism. Environmental racism is when racial beliefs, attitudes, and behaviors are shaped or influenced by one's environment by association and by words. Often, we feel the pressure to conform to our environment. We feel the pressure of conforming to the pressure of family members, the pressure of our affiliations, sororities, fraternities, and groups that we are in. We feel peer pressure when our peers or our associations pressure us with words like, "stay with your own kind."

When I was a child, I can remember walking to school one day and deciding to stop by what we called the icehouse. It was a place where they sold ice and beverages like sodas and beer. They had two water fountains outside, one designated for "colored people" and the other for "white people." I would go to the colored water fountain and I'd drink the water; but I would fantasize about that white water fountain. One day, I noticed no one was around and I jumped over to the white water fountain and drank some of that forbidden water. Now, if you had asked me as a child how did the white-water taste, I would have said it was so good. Now, in my mature years, I realize there was no difference between the white water and the black water. It is all the same. Oftentimes, we are conditioned by environmental pressure and environmental racism.

Our tendency is to conform our beliefs and our attitudes about others and other races by the influence that's placed on us by our environment.

Institutional Racism. Institutional racism is sometimes called structural racism or systemic racism. This virus is somewhat abstract, covert, and subtle. It is like the heart that's hidden. Jeremiah 17:9 says, "The heart is more deceitful than all else and is desperately sick" (NASB). The physical heart that pumps blood throughout our body is hidden, but it is so powerful. In fact, it is so important that when our heart is dysfunctional or diseased, it causes major adverse symptoms throughout our body.

When you talk about racism and you talk about the heart or core of the matter, you have to talk about institutional, systemic racism. This is critical for us to understand.

**Institutional racism happens when racism is a structure.
It is not an event; it is a structure.**

Institutional racism is racism that is a system that functions and goes beyond an individual. It is a group level racism that is structured and has processes, whether it is in government, the school system, the judicial system, business, housing, sports, or entertainment. It is a form of racism that is structured and has processes that reproduces racial inequalities. This structure is both organizational and functions like an organism or virus invading other structures and reproduces itself resulting in destructive processes within the structures it invades.

In her book, "White Fragility," Robin DiAngelo, says, "Institutional racism is collective prejudice backed by legal authority and institutional control. White people in America are the dominant race and there is a gap not only in population between blacks and whites, but between blacks and whites regarding wealth, position, and authority. Institutional control involves position control and authority control. Position control has to do with the fact that white people in America control all the major institutions: business and finance, government, military, media, education, the judicial system, medicine, sports, and entertainment. Authority control is where white people set the laws, policies, practices, and norms that others must live by. [15]

I believe every person, regardless of race or ethnicity, should be proud in a positive way. There should be a sense of unselfish pride about your race. In other words, you shouldn't necessarily want to be in another race. However, if you take racial pride off the table, which group would you want to be a part of? Well, I'm going to answer for you. You would want to be in the group that controls the major insti-

---

15 www.goodreads.com/work/quotes/58159636

tutions and you would want to be in the group that sets the laws, the policies, practices, and norms that others must live by. The reason you would want to be in that group is because you believe being in that group would give you an advantage.

Institutional racism is **a system of advantage based on race**. We could talk about institutional racism in educational inequalities. We could talk about systemic racism in employment, hiring practices, and racial profiling. In the judicial system, and even in the field of entertainment and sports, advantage can be influenced by one's race. This is not just an individual problem, it is a systemic problem, an institutional problem, and a structural problem that goes beyond individuals. In order to change the outcome, we must get to the heart of the matter which is governance, membership, and culture.

Economic Racism. Economic Racism is discrimination based on economic factors that produce racial inequalities. It is discrimination based on job availability beyond minimum wage positions, fair wages, promotion opportunism, availability of goods and needed services, and amount of capital funding for minority business.

Many people believe "everyone has the same opportunities for advancement" and that those individuals need to simply "apply themselves and work hard" and success will come. In the United States, often hailed as "the land of opportunity," this could not be further from the truth for people of color.

Economic disparities between white people and black people can be traced back to discriminatory practices and policies aimed at black people, conscious and unconscious biases in hiring, and more.

For decades, the United States engaged in **redlining** (a practice in which the government and lenders drew red lines on physical maps to deem which areas of a city they would **not** invest in based on whether there was the presence of people of color). Redlined-neighborhood residents would be systematically denied financial services like mortgages, loans (personal and student), credit cards, and insurance. For instance, a financial institution would approve loans for a lower-income white person, but not for a middle-class black person. If a college-educated, hardworking black person lived in one of those neighborhoods (which was inevitable without access to financial services), they did NOT have the same opportunity for advancement as their white counterpart. And although it is now against the law, the effects of these widespread practices are still a current-day reality. White neighborhoods and neighborhoods with less diversity are deemed as more desirable, thus resulting in higher home values and the opportunity to build generational wealth. It is not about actually having generational wealth, but rather about the access and opportunity to build that wealth. So, even if you are not personally wealthy, economic racism allows or denies you the chance to gain it, based on your race.

ASK YOURSELF . . .
- What if your viability for financial services was determined based on your race or the neighborhood you live in, instead of your individual accomplishments and creditworthiness?
- How do you think it would impact you and your family?
- If you have never been impacted by such practices, would you be able to empathize with those who have?

Reactionary Racism. Reactionary racism is what Exodus 21:24 speaks to saying, "an eye for an eye and a tooth for a tooth." Reactionary racism is responding to bias with bias. It is responding to prejudice with prejudice. You hate me, so I hate you back.

🔇

**Reactionary racism is responding to injustices
with violence, retaliation, and generalizations.**

🔇

All white people are not racists. All black people are not violent. All police officers are not abusive.

A Word to Black Christians. You do not have a right to hate anyone regardless of what they do to you. In John 13:34, Jesus says, "a new commandment I give to you, that you love one another; as I have loved you, that you also love one another." This means you must, as a Christian, love and react in love toward everyone, including President Trump. Now, there is a difference between love and respect. You are commanded to love him. You do not have to respect him. The Bible never instructs the believer to respect disrespect. Regardless of our arena of authority, whether you are the President or whether you are a pastor, husband, parent, coach, or anyone on any level of authority, you do not have a right to be disrespectful.

After forty years of pastoring, there have been a few occasions in which I have had to counsel husbands who were demanding respect from their wives when they were operating disrespectfully towards her. They would say things like, "the Bible says the husband is the head of the wife and the wife is to submit to her husband in everything." Ephesians 5 instructs Christians to mutually submit themselves to (serve) one another and then unpacks that mandate by teaching that the wife submits to her own husband and the Church submits to Christ. Ephesians 5:25 reveals that the husband must love the wife the way Christ loved the Church. Please understand that when the Bible says to the wife to submit to her husband in everything, she is submitting in love but not submitting to abuse or disrespect.

Here's the irrefutable truth or bottom line: "Be not deceived, God is not mocked whatsoever a man soweth, that shall he reap" (Galatians 6:7 KJV).

A Word to White Christians. I'm not attacking him, but President Trump sows a lot of disrespect. Over his history, and especially the last few years he's been in office, he has constantly called people disrespectful, disparaging names. He calls people low life, horse-faced, slime balls, total losers, slobs, and dumb. Who does that? Does authority give us the right to call people disparaging names? He insults ethnic groups.

President Trump has called African nations, "s***hole nations." He called black athletes that were legally protesting SOBs. He told four congresswomen who are people of color and three of them were born in America to go back to where they came from. He blasted an entire Baltimore district, the majority being African American, and he said concerning the district that it is a "disgusting, rat and rodent infested mess, it's a filthy place." How would you feel if your leader and your President talked about the place you live like that? That's disrespect and God does not instruct us, as Christians, to respect disrespect.

I'm challenging white Christians to see such attacks as disrespect because they're cheering President Trump on and think he is being bold when such comments are simply racist. As white Christians, it's **complicit** to laugh and cheer when someone is being mean and disrespectful of others. The Scripture is very clear at this point. We are commanded to be kind to one another (Ephesians 4:32). Sowing kindness reaps kindness. Sowing disrespect reaps disrespect.

ASK YOURSELF . . .
- Does authority give you the right to call people disparaging names, insult ethnic groups, or disrespect others with whom you disagree?
- As a Christian, how should you respond if you are treated in this way?

As a Christian, you are to respond based on Scripture. The Scripture teaches us that we can be angry but sin not (Ephesians 4:26). There's nothing wrong with your anger, but you must channel your anger in a proper way, in a positive way. The Bible says be angry but when your anger is unresolved and is channeled in an improper way, then you end up in bitterness and that bitterness will spring up and trouble you and will defile the people around you (Hebrews 12:15). The Bible also says that the wrath of man does not work the righteousness of God (James 1:20). In other words, unresolved anger, bitterness, and hate hinders you as a Christian from moving forward, and it hinders God from working in your life.

As I have said before, as believers, we are warned by the Lord Himself to be careful how we use our words. Biblical, proverbial wisdom warns that death and life are in the power of the tongue. In Matthew 12:33-37, Jesus says when a good man has a good deposit of his heart, through his words, he will bring forth good things, but an evil man and carnal man out of the evil deposit of his heart through his words will bring forth evil things. Jesus warned that every idle word that a man speaks he will give account of it in the day of judgment and by our words we are justified, by our words we are condemned. The Scripture mandates that we are to let no corrupt communication come out of our mouths, but instead, we are to be kind to one another.

In James 3:5, it says that the tongue is a fire. It says that it is a world of iniquity, it sets on fire the course of nature. Then in verse 10, it says out of the mouth proceeds blessings and cursing, these things ought not to be. James concludes by letting us know what wisdom we are to follow as Christians. He says the wisdom that is carnal, the wisdom that is fleshly, the wisdom that is devilish, causes strife, division, confusion, and it causes instability. However, there is a wisdom that comes from above that is pure (see James 3:13-18) and will help us as Christians to deal with the **Social Viruses of Racism**.

This wisdom from above is not a mixture of speaking good and speaking bad. It is peaceable and it builds bridges not divisions. The Bible says this wisdom is gentle, it is kind, it is easy to be entreated, and it is not stubborn. It is full of mercy, it is full of good fruits, and it has no hypocrisy and no prejudice in it. Biblical truth is that we are to be led by the Word regardless who we are and to whom we are speaking.

We are to be led as Christians by God's Word.

I am talking to and challenging the Body of Christ; Jesus said that we are to be **the salt** of the earth. We are the seasoning, the flavor. We are to preserve. We are to prevent corruption in the earth. However, Jesus says if the salt has lost its savor, if it has lost its voice, He says that it is good for nothing but to be cast out and trodden by the foot of men (see Matthew 5:13).

ASK YOURSELF . . .
- Have we lost our savor?
- Have we lost our voice?
- Are we in danger of being cast out as being good for nothing?

Too often we have politicized the Church. We have also politicized our relationship with God and we have moved from being a voice to being a vote.

REFLECTION STEPS
Begin by reviewing the Scriptures presented in this chapter, specifically the ones listed below. Study them in light of the questions presented to us as the Church and the Body of Christ. Record your insights.

1 Corinthians 1:10	Acts 13:1
John 17:21-23	Jeremiah 16:19b
Psalm 133:1-3	Jeremiah 17:9

Exodus 21:24   Matthew 12:33-37
Jeremiah 17:9   James 3:3-18
Galatians 6:7

Then review these Power Points set apart in Chapter 2:

Generational racism is really the result of
negative racial ethnic socialization.

Our tendency is to conform our beliefs and our attitudes
about others and other races
by the influence that's placed on us by our environment.

Institutional racism is when racism is a structure.
It is not an event; it is a structure.

Economic racism is not about actually having
generational wealth, but rather about the
access and opportunity to build that wealth.

Reactionary racism is responding to injustices
with violence, retaliation, and generalizations.

Do you disagree with any of these? Why?

Dare to Confront with the Truth and Act Justly

As you read through these Power Points, what did God "dare" you to do to begin to "unmute" the members of the Body of Christ that may be living under the influence of these **Social Viruses of Racism?**

_____

_____

_____

Record in a journal the response you received. Continue praying for revelation for each of these people.

Chapter 3
History Matters

"The purpose of studying history is not to deride human action, nor to weep over it or hate it, but to understand it. And hopefully then to learn from it as we contemplate our future." — Nelson Mandela [16]

Someone sent me an article that was posted online recently. This really was very enlightening, and a very beautiful example of what God is doing in our Country. The Alabama Department of Archives and History, in a statement of recommitment dated June 23, 2020, declared:

> "Systemic racism remains a reality in American society, despite belief in racial equality on the part of most individuals. Historically, our government, our economy, and many private institutions seeded or perpetuated discrimination against racial minorities to the political, economic, and social advantage of

---

16 www.goodreads.com/quotes/tag/history

whites. The decline of overt bigotry in mainstream society has not erased the legacy of blatant racist systems that operated for hundreds of years."

The leadership of the Alabama Department of Archives and History should be commended for the bold and honest acknowledgment in their statement of recommitment. This is a classic illustration of the move of God moving on the hearts of institutions in our Country and around the world.

No person can have a deep, honest, relevant, and transformative discussion without a knowledge of history.

I BELIEVE . . .
- God will make some powerful connections to solve this problem across denominational and racial lines.
- The Church will have powerful engagements and discussions about race.
- Christians will link arms and hearts together in unity based on the irrefutable truths of the Scriptures and step away from myths, half-truths and lies rooted in generational and systemic racism.

We cannot have deep transformative discussions, though, without a knowledge of history. In this chapter, we are going to talk about slavery, white Christianity, and genuine Christianity.

Slavery. Too many people mistakenly believe God does not have a clear position on slavery. Exodus 21:16 declares, "He that stealeth a man, not a thing, not property, but he that stealeth a man and selleth him or if he be found in his hands, he shall surely be put to death" (KJV paraphrased).

Now, I don't how you feel, but I am convicted by strong words concerning slavery. In Deuteronomy 24:7, we read, "If a man be found stealing any of his brethren of the children of Israel and make merchandise of him, turn him into property, or selleth him then that thief shall die and they put evil away from among you" (KJV paraphrased).

When you review and analyze these divine declarations, these statements use critically important words about stealing. God declares that:

- Slavery is stealing.
- Merchandising a person, selling a person, is stealing.
- Slavery is using people and loving money instead of loving people and using money.
- Slavery is treating people who are made in God's image as stuff; it's dehumanizing.
- God calls slavery evil.

What was slavery? Slavery was a system deliberately structured to produce a plantation mentality. Slavery was designed by a racist mindset to create five things.

1. Slavery was designed to create a doctrine of inferiority.
2. Slavery imparts a sense of inadequacy in a person.
3. Slavery instills a negative self-concept.
4. Slavery systemically develops dependency on a "superior" race.
5. Slavery ethnically and racially separates and divides people.

As I began to study this theme of slavery, I learned that there was what I'm calling a co-conspiracy. Genuine Christianity and uncompromised preaching of God's Word presented a barrier in the minds of the slave owners and Christian missionaries who were trying to justify slavery and racial prejudice. Men had to somehow quiet their consciences to engage in slavery. So, in order to enforce this prejudicial blight, two tools were used to erect a barrier or wall of separation between whites and blacks.

The Tool of Legislation. Those who were creating this system of slavery were concerned about slaves becoming Christians because there was an unwritten law that Christians could not be held as slaves. Consequently, if blacks were allowed to be converted, then they could not be held as slaves. Now, that was the problem for the slave owner. Christian missionaries were motivating the slave owners to allow the slaves to become Christians, but the slave owners were concerned about the slave being emancipated once he became a Christian.

To get around this dilemma, laws were enacted that stated conversion did not lead to a release of servitude. Such laws are unbiblical and completely sinister. In fact, there were all kinds of laws enacted during the days of slavery. It was illegal for slaves to read and write. It was against the law for slaves to congregate. It was against the law for slaves to own and sell property. It was unlawful for slaves to become citizens, vote, and hold office. It was against the law for slaves to have firearms. There were all kinds of black codes after the Civil War, and then there were the Jim Crow laws that legalized segregation. In order to institutionalize slavery in America, legislation had to take place.

In 1667, the Virginia General Assembly enacted a law that baptism and conversion to Christianity did not alter the condition of slaves nor release them from servitude.

The Tool of the Bible. There was also the tool of the slave Bible. In 1807, the slave Bible was created and produced in England. It was a redacted version of the Bible. It had all of the references to freedom, escape, and equality removed. This redacted version of the Bible, this slave Bible, kept all the parts of the Bible that dealt with submission and obedience to authority.

Meanwhile in America, white preachers acted in accordance and entered into a partnership with slave owners. They believed that preaching edited portions of the Bible would make slaves better workers and serve as security against rebellion. Here is a very unfortunate reality, slavery in America lasted for 246 years. It existed and persisted so long because the white Church sanctioned slavery and gave permission or approval to slave owners to practice slavery and at the same time call themselves Christians. This next important Power Point is the key to not only dismantling slavery, but also to the dismantling of systemic racism or institutional racism in America today.

If legislation and an edited, distorted version of the Bible justified and nailed down slavery into society, then it would take both legislation and the uncompromised Truth of the whole Bible to lift slavery off society.

That is the purposeful goal of this book. Two essentials are needed today to disarm and destroy racism in the Church and ultimately in our culture.

First, we must create just legislation. Necessary change must be made in our culture's laws and policies. We must have a change in our cultural mindset. That change must happen through legislation. If our attitudes and actions are to change in America, we must change our laws and legislate just practices in government, business, education, entertainment, religion, and the media. For example, racist propaganda promoting violence and murder in the media or entertainment must be illegal.

However, this is not my arena. Secondly as Christians, we must purpose to challenge the Church to speak out against racism and to practice reconciliation and unity because it is going to take the uncompromised preaching of God's whole Word to dismantle both cultural and religious racism in the Church.

White Christianity. Slavery gave birth to what has been called white Christianity. White Christianity maintains the belief in both the inferiority of the black race and segregation. During the days of post-Civil War, freed slaves were allowed to become Christians, but they were never viewed as equals. Even though they were in the Church and worshipping in the same building, they were never allowed to worship together. They were always in segregated spaces. In other words, the black members of the Church had to either sit in the balcony or they had to sit in the back.

They were never viewed as equals, consequently, they could not hold leadership positions. In our last chapter, I said that the white Church and the black Church were a perversion, an alteration, and a distortion of God's original intent or original plan for the Church. I also said that this division in the Body of Christ is a social construct and a human invented classification system. God never intended for there to be a Black Church, a White Church, a Hispanic Church, a Native American, or an Asian American Church. God intended for His Body to be one.

Now, post-Civil War black people desired to be in a worship environment where they would have freedom of expression. They wanted to participate and be developed as leaders, but the white Christian Church was unwilling to allow black people to integrate into leadership or integrate into the freedom of expression. Consequently, the Black Church was birthed out of the White Christianity's unwillingness to treat the Black Christian as equals created in the image of God.

Once the Black Church was instituted, black people were developed and allowed to grow in leadership. There were black leaders like Absalom Jones who founded the African Episcopal Church of St. Thomas, Richard Allen who founded the AME Church, and then all these other great leaders like, Martin Luther King Jr. who were birthed and allowed to develop out of a Black Church. I was not saying that there is no benefit and there is no goodness in the Black Church. I was saying that it was never God's intent for there to be segregation in His Body. He intended for His Body to be perfectly joined in unity.

After what we can call the religious liberation of black people, came the black power movement of the 1960s and 1970s that emphasized racial pride, economic empowerment, and black self-determination. Some people in the black power movement called Christianity the white man's religion because they saw the hypocrisy in the Church. However, what they were experiencing was never genuine Christianity. I believe that there are still vestiges of White Christianity in today's Church, but what we need is genuine Christianity throughout the Christian Church. We must think, feel and act as One in Christ, renewed in mind and heart.

Genuine Christianity. The infant Church in Paul's day was under the umbrella of Rome. Close to 90 percent of the population in Rome were slaves. There were approximately sixty million slaves. However, slavery in Rome was different than slavery in America. Slavery in Rome was not about skin color. It was really about captives of war and people who had sold themselves because of their indebtedness. The entire economy in Rome was built on slave labor. Instead of challenging the Church to revolt against slavery, which would have destroyed the infant Church.

Paul attacked the institution of slavery at its spiritual root. Many people today think that the writings of Paul endorsed and supported slavery. However, Paul understood that Christianity was in its infancy and if he had encouraged this young infant Church to rebel and burn down Rome and loot all those things, he knew that Christianity would be stamped out quickly. He brought genuine Christianity to Rome and preached the uncompromised gospel to both the Christian slave owners and the slaves.

When you read the New Testament letters by the Apostle Paul, and especially, those parts of the letters in Colossians and Ephesians where slave and slave-master relationships are mentioned, remember, Paul is not talking to the unsaved. He is talking to both the Christian slave owner and to the Christian slave. In John 8:32, Jesus says, "You will know the truth and the truth will make you free." In 2 Corinthians 3:17, it says, "Where the Spirit of the Lord is, there is liberty."

I want to explain how the Apostle Paul challenged slavery. I have on a shirt with buttons on it. I am also wearing a coat that has buttons on it. If you want to take the buttons off this coat or off my shirt, you can either grab the button and tear it off or you can unravel the threads and the button will fall off. Now, it is better if you want to take this button off the coat or off the shirt to unravel the threads than it is to snatch the button off. If you tear the button off, then you will actually tear the jacket or the shirt, but **if you loosen the thread, then the button will fall off without any damage** to the shirt or coat. That's how the Apostle Paul approached the issue of slavery. He took the uncompromised gospel and he unraveled the threads of slavery by preaching both to the Christian slave master and to the Christian slave.

The Bible provides insight on how to unravel the thread of slavery. These same insights can be leveraged to dismantle racism in America and in the Church.

The Thread of Slavery	<<vs>>	The Gospel
Disrespect	Ephesians 6:9	Respect (mutual)
Harsh Treatment	Ephesians 6:9	Kindness (forbear threatening)
Superiority	Ephesians 6:9	Impartiality (God doesn't put one above another)
Inequality	Galatians 3:28	Equality
Unfair Treatment	Ephesians 6:9	Respect (mutual)
Non-personhood (not considered a person)	Philemon 15-16	True Brotherhood

I've identified six threads of slavery: 1) Disrespect, 2) Harsh Treatment, 3) Superiority, 4) Inequality, 5) Unfair Treatment, and 6) Nonpersonhood.

The first three are found in Ephesians 6:9. As Paul went into these areas and preached to the Christian slave masters and to the Christian slave, he was unraveling those threads, one by one. "And, **ye masters, do the same things unto them, forbearing threatening**: knowing that your Master also is in heaven; **neither is there respect of persons with him** (KJV emphasis added)."

He told the Christian slave master to "do the same things unto them," to do likewise to them. In other words, the thread of slavery is **disrespect.** But, if the slave master does likewise, then that is **mutual respect**. You cannot have mutual respect and have slavery. You cannot operate in mutual respect and operate in racism. It then moves to the next thread of slavery which is **harsh treatment**. He told the slave master to forbear threatening. The Amplified Bible expounds by saying, "give up threatening *and* abusive words." This means if the slave master forbears threatening, he must treat the slave with **kindness**. You cannot operate in kindness toward someone and treat them harshly either through words or actions. The final thread in this verse unravels **superiority.** The Apostle Paul went on to say to the slave masters, "knowing that your Master in heaven neither is there no respect of persons with Him" (KJV). He is teaching the slave masters that God shows **impartiality**, that "Your Father in Heaven doesn't put one person above another." Paul is telling the slave master to look at God. That unravels the thread of superiority.

We find the next thread, **inequality**, in Galatians 3:28. Paul writes, "There is neither Jew nor Gentile; there is neither bond nor free; there is neither female nor male, but **you are all one in Christ**" (KJV). He is telling the slave master and the slave, you are one. In other words, he is preaching **equality**. You cannot have slavery if you have equality.

In Colossians 4:1, Paul said to the slave masters, "Master give to the slave what is just and equal" (KJV). Now, this is a part of Paul's instructions that the slave Bible edited out. A thread of slavery is unfair treatment. If the slave master obeys Paul in Colossians 4:1, then he must treat the slave with fairness and justice; so that thread of unfair treatment is unraveled.

The final thread of slavery is **non-personhood** where the slave was considered property and not a person. While in Rome, Paul met a runaway slave, Onesimus, and led him to Christ. Onesimus partnered in ministry with the Apostle Paul. Paul told Philemon, the slave's master, "I am sending Onesimus back to you." Was Paul sending Onesimus back to become a slave? Absolutely not. He said, "I'm sending him back to you but receive him not as a slave but above a slave, receive him as a brother beloved in the flesh" (Philemon 15-16). In other words, to paraphrase what Paul was saying, "I don't want you to receive him as a slave, don't receive him as property, instead, receive him as a man, as a brother in the Lord." The Amplified Bible reads, " . . . receive him not as a slave any longer." Paul sent the slave back to Philemon so that Philemon would emancipate him (set him free from legal and social restrictions), remove that slave label off him, and he could be a free man. Paul is preaching **true brotherhood**.

Remember I said that there was an unwritten law that a Christian could not be held as a slave. I believe that Philemon gives us insight to where this unwritten law came from. Paul was preaching emancipation. He was not preaching go back and be a good slave.

Christianity fully embraced and fully lived out equals equality.
Christianity is not white Christianity, but genuine Christianity.
Racism fully embraced and fully lived out,
equals inferiority and superiority.

REFLECTION STEPS

Begin by reviewing the Scriptures presented in this chapter, specifically the ones listed below. Study them in the light of the questions confronting us as the Church and the Body of Christ. Record your insights.

Exodus 21:16
Deuteronomy 24:7
John 8:32
2 Corinthians 3:17
Ephesians 6:9
Galatians 3:28
Colossians 4:1
Philemon 15-16

Then review these Power Points set apart in Chapter 3.

No person can have a deep, honest, relevant,
and transformative discussion without a knowledge of history.

If legislation and an edited, distorted version of the Bible
justified and nailed down slavery into society,
it will take both legislation and the uncompromised truth
of the whole Bible to lift slavery off society.

Christianity fully embraced and fully lived out equals equality.
Christianity is not white Christianity, but genuine Christianity.
Racism fully embraced and fully lived out,
equals inferiority and superiority.

Dare to Confront with the Truth and Act Justly

As you read through these Power Points, what did God "dare" you to do to begin to "unmute" the members of the Body of Christ that may be living under misconceptions concerning Slavery, White Christianity, and Genuine Christianity.

Perhaps, use these questions:
- Is what I see in the Church genuine Christianity or is it white Christianity?
- How do I view other Christians of different races?
- Do I view them as inferior or do I see them as equals?

Pray and ask God to show you the first steps He wants you to take with each of the people you have listed.

_____

_____

_____

Record in a journal the response you received. Continue praying for revelation for each of these people.

Chapter 4
History Matters
— Present-Day Realities

No person. can have a deep, honest, relevant, and transformative discussion without knowledge. If there is going to be a deep, transparent kind of discussion to make progress in this area of racial equality or racial reconciliation, we must have knowledge.

As we continue our search for knowledge, we are going to delve into black self-hate, white folk looting, and "dog whistle politics." There are three themes that are going to run through each of these three areas of study.

1. **Accountability.** Accountability creates trust and support. A lack of accountability erodes trust and destroys support.
2. **Psychological vestiges.** We are going to look for traces of the past that are evident in the present, and apart from interruption, will be evident in our future.
3. **Seed sowing consequences.** Finally, we are going to be dealing with the consequences of the seed we sow. Galatians 6:7-8

in the Message Bible, reads, "Don't be misled, no one makes a fool of God. What a person plants, he will harvest. The person who plants selfishness, ignoring the needs of others, ignoring God, will reap a harvest of weeds."

Black Self-hate. Self-hate is what I call a "plantation mentality." We will compare the history of American slavery with our present-day realities in the black community as we look for psychological vestiges. Remember, we are talking about blacks as a group, and we are talking about whites as a group. When we look at American slavery, we see that slavery programmed male slaves to be irresponsible. When we look over into the present reality, we find that more than 70 percent of African American children are raised by single mothers. Male slaves were studs whose job was to make baby slaves and women slaves were treated as sex objects. Our present reality when we are talking about accountability, some black men are still acting like studs who rarely form lasting relationships with women and women are treated as sexual objects in movies, videos, and entertainment.

In American slavery, slaves were taught to devalue life. When we look at our present reality, we see a rise in black-on-black crime. Our fourth situation in American slavery is we find lighter skinned slaves with features closer to the master were treated better. In our present reality, beauty is still based on color of skin, hair texture, and facial features.

In American slavery, slaves were discouraged from uniting. Slaves were rewarded for snitching. Slaves were pitted against one another. Light-skinned slaves were pitted against dark-skinned slaves. In slavery times, there were two kinds of slaves on the plantation—the house slaves and the field slaves. Slave owners would strategically cause the field slaves to be in division and opposed to the house slaves. Jealousy and envy existed between the two, and the slave owners never wanted them to work together. When we look at our present reality, some blacks struggle working with other blacks and talk against other successful blacks due to jealousy. Goods and services created by blacks are believed by other blacks to be inferior.

In American slavery, literacy and intelligence were outlawed. When we look at our present reality, some of our kids ridicule other kids for being smart. In American slavery, slaves were given the worst food and the leftovers. In our present reality, I think some black movie producers, black music producers, and black comedians are still giving black people what I call "plantation food." Movies and music that are full of profanity, sexual exploitation, and full of things that are not uplifting instead of movies and music that inspire us like "Hidden Figures" and "Harriet."

I have seen these same themes, generational curses, and plantation mentality behaviors in the Church. I see black pastors talking against other black pastors. I see church members talking against other church members. I see church members who get upset when other black church members crossover into white congregations, and I see black Christians who crossover into white congregations turn around and talk against black churches. I call this a "plantation mentality."

Jesus said, "Thou shalt love thy neighbor as thyself" (Matthew 19:19 KJV). That is a commandment which tells me that love begins on the inside of us. We must respect ourselves.

"People who hate themselves are not psychologically equipped to function as equals and potent members of any society."[17]

It is important that we love ourselves. When I think about this plantation mentality, I think of one word and that is the "N" word. We have black people using the most racially offensive word in the history of America toward black people. There are black youth using the "N"

---

word in their everyday conversation with other black people. Sometimes, I wonder if we understand what the "N" word stands for.

The "N" word was the watch word of the slave owners. The "N" word meant to the slave owner a black person. It was used to insult, it was used to injure, and it distinguished black people from white people. The "N" word was used to communicate that black people are innately ignorant, uncivilized, an inferior race, and not human. I believe that if black people understood the origin of the "N" word, they would eradicate it from their vocabulary. In fact, I believe that we should remove this word out of our vocabulary.

Here's the bottom line, we black people, have to do a better job of respecting and loving our own selves. We must do a better job of respecting and loving other black people.

ASK YOURSELF . . .

* *Do I have a plantation mentality?*

I was talking to one of my sons in the faith, and I am paraphrasing something he had heard. He said a young white lady was discussing race with her white mother. Apparently, the young white girl felt that this issue of racial equality and racial injustice was very important. It was as if she was trying to get her mother on board, but her mother said, "Black people need to treat themselves better and when they treat themselves better, then we will treat them better." That is an illegitimate excuse. How we treat ourselves does not legitimize white people being racist, but it does make us think. It does cause us to think that we need to hold ourselves accountable for how we behave and how we operate, especially toward each other.

🔇

We have to seek to obey
Jesus' command in Matthew 19:19,
"Thou shalt love thy neighbor as thyself" (KJV).

🔇

White Folk Looting. The word "loot" means to sack; it means to rob of value by capture. The word "looting" also means to despoil, to strip of belongings things that belong to others. Thirdly, the word "loot" means to remove, to take things away by force. All of us have watched television, especially during this time of national and international protests regarding racial injustices and inequalities. We have all looked at people looting stores and looting businesses.

For all of us honest, caring, decent people, whether you are black or white, we struggle with looting. We all struggle seeing people break into stores and steal things that belong to others. We all believe that those who loot should be held accountable. Looting and violence undermine future progress. It moves the narrative and the focus from change to unrest.

I want to give you a different twist on looting by taking you through biblical history, world history, and American history to see how white people looted, despoiled, and removed precious things from black people.

BIBLICAL HISTORY

When we talk about biblical history, the Bible is a multicultural, a multiracial revelation. In other words, there are black people mentioned in the Old Testament and black people mentioned in the New Testament. However, most of us have never heard about the black people in Scripture because white people looted biblical history from black people.

When we look in the Old Testament, we see black people throughout biblical history.

- **Nimrod.** In Genesis 10, we meet Nimrod, a black man who was a brilliant empire builder who built the city of Babylon.
- **Jethro.** In Exodus 19, Jethro, Moses' father-in-law, mentor, and counselor was a black man.
- **Hobab**, in Numbers 10, was Jethro's son, and he was Moses' scout through the wilderness.
- **Queen of Sheba.** In I Kings 10, we have a black queen, the Queen of Sheba.
- **Zephaniah**, who wrote an Old Testament book, was a black man. Zephaniah 1:1, says, "The Word of the Lord which came to Zephaniah, the son of Cushi . . . " Cushi means "Ethiopian" or "blackness."

Now, it is interesting that in history there was so much talk against interracial connections. Henry Louis Gates Jr., in his book, "Stony the Road," said, "Miscegenation or the mixing of races was the white supremacist's nightmare." [18] Yet, when we look at the Scripture, we see Abraham, Moses, Joseph, and David were married to black women.

Then, when we move over into the New Testament, we meet these black Christians:

- **Simon of Cyrene** in Mark 15, who helped bear Jesus' cross was a black man.
- **Alexander and Rufus**, in Mark 15 and Romans 16, were two sons of Simon of Cyrene.
- **Ethiopian eunuch.** In Acts 8, we have the Ethiopian eunuch, who was a black man, a man of great authority under the queen

---

18 Published April 2, 2019 by Penguin Press, https://www.goodreads.com/book/show/40909438-stony-the-road

of Ethiopia.

- **Simeon**, called Niger, and **Lucius** of Cyrene in Acts 13 were prophets or teachers in the first Christian Church.
- **Simon**, the Canaanite in Matthew 10, one of the twelve apostles, who was a descendant of Ham.

WORLD HISTORY

Let's move from biblical history to world history. Black people were taught that they were uncivilized, ignorant, incapable of learning, and incapable of leading, but when we look at world history and we remove all of the racism and all of the looting, we see that ancient Egypt was known as the land of Ham, the father of the black race. Psalm 105:23 says Israel also came into Egypt and Jacob sojourned in the land of Ham. Ancient Egypt was known as the land of Ham. The descendants of Ham, people of color, ruled most of the known world for the first 2,000 years of world history.

People of color were the most advanced people on the earth. They were building empires and organizing governments. The ancient Egyptians were people of color. They were proficient in mathematics, medicine, engineering, and architecture. The great pyramids, one of the seven wonders of the world, were built by people of color. People of color gave the world what has become modern calculus. Egyptians' advancements in education were known around the world. Moses was educated by black people.

AMERICAN HISTORY

White people looted black people of biblical history, world history, and American history. I want to focus for a moment on American history. Let me give you an assignment. The next time you are in a bookstore or in a library, I want you to go to the history section for books about black Americans. Ask the person who waits on you if they carry any books on black American history. I went to one of the major bookstores and I asked the cashier if they any books on black American history. She took me back to the history section, walked past all the books to a little section called Black American History.

Very few people know about black inventors. For example, the refrigeration unit was invented by Frederick Jones, the clothes dryer by G.T. Sampson, the automatic gear shift by Ricard Spikes, the fire extinguisher by T. Marshall, dry cleaning by Thomas Jenning, the gas mask by Garrett Morgan, the modern lawn mower by L.A. Burr, blood banks by Dr. Charles Richard Drew, automatic opening and closing elevator doors by Alexander Miles, Laserphaco Probe and cataract surgery procedures by Dr. Patricia Bath.

George Washington Carver invented hundreds of uses of the peanut. The pioneer of open-heart surgery was Daniel Hale Williams. The interesting thing about all these inventions is they are things that we use and are familiar to us and they were invented by people of color. In the post-Civil War, free slaves didn't have the resources to patent their inventions or the finances to support their business ideas, so whites took credit for them.

Think about all the great baseball players in the Negro League who were kept out of the record books because they were banded from major league baseball. When I mention Oscar Charleston, Josh Gibson, John Henry "Pop" Lloyd, "Cool" Papa Bell, and Buck Leonard, I'm convinced most of you have never heard of them because they were great African American baseball players who could only play in the Negro League. Consider what would have happened if they had been allowed in the major league. Satchel Paige eventually played in major league baseball, but I think he was in his forties by then. What if he had been allowed to play in the major league in his prime? Think about the record books, all the people who hold records in major league baseball. How would that have changed if black players were allowed to play in the majors?

I used to love Elvis who was designated as the king of rock and roll, but where did Elvis get his dance moves from?

🔇

Much of what we call American history is incomplete, and in some cases, untrue.

🔇

The facts will rock your emotional boat. Think about the inspiration, wealth, and fame that was stolen from black people. Consider all the famous men and women who have never heard themselves mentioned in the history books. Think about all the years that we took American history classes and there was no mention of black people. Think of all the black kids who now think that the only way they can be successful is in athletics because they never heard about these black inventors and were never taught about what people of color have achieved in history. These kids have lost that sense of inspiration all because black people were looted.

Now, I am not in any way trying to get you as a white person to feel guilty. I am not in any way saying that you personally robbed black people. I am trying to inform you so that at the very least, you will have empathy.

"Dog Whistle Politics"

With all lowliness and gentleness, with longsuffering, bearing with one another in love, endeavoring to keep the unity of the Spirit in the bond of peace. There is one body and one Spirit, just as you were called in one hope of your calling; one Lord, one faith, one baptism.
(Ephesians 4:2-5)

What this is saying to us as Christians, whether we are black, white, red, yellow or brown, it is important for us to endeavor for unity and peace in the Body of Christ. The word *endeavor* means to labor. In other words, all Christians are **to labor to keep unity and a bond of peace.**

As we navigate through the politicized world we live in, it is going to be critical for us to see anything that would divide us, which leads me to what I call, "dog whistle politics." Dog whistle politics divides and stokes resentment. When it has a racial bent, it divides races and stokes resentment between races.

Dog whistle politics clandestinely solicit and rally certain people using certain phrases that resonate with the target audience. We could say that dog whistle political agendas contain coded racial appeal. It contains a political strategy, statement, appeal, or slogan that conveys a controversial second message that is understood only by those who support the message.

ASK YOURSELF . . .

- *When I hear the words or the phrase, "law and order," what does that mean and who is the target audience?*
- *When I hear the words "war on drugs," what does that mean and who is the target audience?*
- *When I hear "war on terror," do I think of those of Arab or Muslim descent?*
- *What do I think when I hear "make America great again?" What does "again" mean? Who is the target audience? What was lost that we need to get back?"*

**As we navigate through our politicized world,
it is critical that we, as Christians,
not allow ourselves to be divided or
allow ourselves to be separated by dog whistle politics.**

For example, think about the present debate in America over the removal of confederate flags, confederate monuments, and names from army bases, streets, and college buildings. Why is it important to remove these things? Some say the confederate monuments and flags represent service, sacrifice, heritage, and southern values. Others say that the confederate flags and monuments represent the ownership of slaves, the superiority of the white race, and the inferiority of the black race.

When we look at NASCAR, who banned the confederate flag, why did they ban it? Should they have banned it?

When we look at the state of Mississippi that retired a state flag that had confederate emblems. What is this all about?

President Trump said it is about our heritage, our history, our culture, and the greatness of our Country. When they vandalize our beautiful statues, they are vandalizing our history. Is this dog whistle politics?

If we are going to take the statues down, if we are going to remove the flag, we need to at least know why we are doing it. We need to know should it stay up. So, I decided that I was going to take the time to study it out myself. I discovered that the confederacy was a collection of eleven states that seceded or broke away from the U.S. in 1860 following the election of Abraham Lincoln. These states were convinced that white supremacy and the institution of slavery was threatened by the election of Abraham Lincoln.

I discovered that Jefferson Davis, who served as president of the confederacy, said, "America was founded by white men for white men."[19] In a speech known today as the Cornerstone Address, the vice president of the confederacy, Alexander H. Stephens, described the confederacy and the confederate ideology as being centrally based, and he said, "Upon the great truth that the Negro is not equal to the white man, that slavery, subordination to the superior race is his, the black man's, natural and normal condition. We went to war to protect our property."[20] The Civil War that lasted four years with between 600 to 800 thousand people killed, he said was to protect our property.

For four years, the confederacy was a repressive, pro-slavery nation devoted to white supremacy and a nation that was at war against the United States. The statues, flags, and names represent their purpose and were to preserve the memory of the cause and the people who fought and died for that cause.

ASK YOURSELF . . .

- *As a Bible-believing Christian, do I believe we should preserve the emblems, symbols, names, statues, monuments, and flags that represented the cause of white supremacy and the cause of the subordination of black people?*

In the biblical history, Josiah was the sixteenth king of Judah. He inherited a kingdom full of idolatry, immorality, violence, and ignorance. Josiah is called the great reformer and he did three things. He cleansed the temple from all objects of pagan worship and removed all sanctuaries built to pagan worship. He centralized worship in Jerusalem. Then, he found the lost Torah, the Word of God, and promoted it. So, we see a reformer in scripture realized that before he could promote the Word of God, he had to cleanse and remove some things.

---

19 www.azquotes.com/author/3716-Jefferson_Davis

20 www.azquotes.com/author/42738-Alexander_H_Stephens#:~:text=Alexander%20H.%20Ste

WALKING THROUGH A MINEFIELD

Discussing racism can be like walking through a mine field. Sometimes, nations build minefields that separate them from the enemy. As one walks through the minefield, the mines explode. The discussion on racism is like that. It is like walking through a mine field. Sometimes, you have some explosions from black people when you talk about self-hate. You could have explosions sometimes when you talk about white folk looting. Then, I talked about dog whistle politics and sometimes we have our idols, and it can cause an explosion when racism is discussed. However, we must talk about it.

Maybe my assignment is to bring to the surface these difficult discussions. We will never have racial equality if we don't deal with these difficult and profound discussions. We must be transparent and open and talk about some of these things. Maybe my assignment is to simply give you information, give you concepts, and give you history that will enable, equip, and give you the resources and knowledge base to begin the difficult discussions that we must have. The important thing to remember is if we can get through the mine field, we can unmute the muted voice of the Church.

I think about my relationship with my wife. My wife and I have been married over forty-two years. That's a long time. I have a wonderful marriage and my wife is my very best friend on planet earth. There's nobody on the planet I would rather be with than my wife. I love her. However, early in our marriage, we struggled in our relationship. We weren't sure we had made the right decision. We said things to each other that were strong and harsh in some cases. We got angry at each other at times. There were times I didn't want to go home, and she didn't want me to come home. There were times when we both questioned whether we should have gotten married.

However, the thing we had going for us was we always talked. It wasn't always nice what we said. We weren't always cool when we said it. We weren't always respectful when we said it, but we always talked.

We talked and kept talking and we said what we felt. I said what I felt about her, and it wasn't always kind. She said what she felt about me, and it wasn't always kind. She got angry sometimes. I got angry sometimes. She got upset and I got upset sometimes, but we kept talking and we talked our way into a place of agreement.

What am I saying? I am saying blacks, whites, and other minorities are going to need to have those hard, difficult, transparent discussions that don't make us feel good. We may get angry; we may not say it right; we may have to come back and apologize, but we have to talk. We must talk and that is what the Spirit of God said to me. He said, a muted voice is no voice.

REFLECTION STEPS

Begin by reviewing the biblical, world, and American history presented in this chapter. Record your insights.

_____

_____

_____

_____

_____

_____

Then review these Power Points set apart in Chapter 4.

We have to seek to obey what Jesus said in Matthew 19:19,
"Thou shalt love thy neighbor as thyself" (KJV).
As we navigate through our politicized world,
it is critical that we, as Christians,
not allow ourselves to be divided or
allow ourselves to be separated by dog whistle politics.

Much of what we call American history is incomplete,
and in some cases, untrue.

Dare to Confront with the Truth and Act Justly

As you read through these Power Points, what did God "dare" you to do to begin to "unmute" the members of the Body of Christ that may be living under the wrong historical information.

_____

_____

_____

_____

_____

_____

Pray and ask God to show you the first steps He wants you to take with each of the people you have listed.

Record in a journal the response you received. Continue praying for revelation for each of these people.

Chapter 5

The Unmuted Voice

Silence is complicit. The word *complicit* means to be involved with others in an illegal activity or to be involved with others in a wrongdoing. To be complicit and say nothing are a form of **passive racism**. In discussing passive and active racist behavior, Psychologist Beverly Daniel Tatum said, "I sometimes visualize the ongoing cycle of racism as a moving walkway at the airport."[21]

Like me, you have probably walked on that moving walkway at the airport. Sometimes, I get on that walkway and I'm tired, so I just STAND and let the walkway take me on down. Other times, I'm in a hurry, so I get on the same moving walkway at the airport and instead of just standing, I WALK AND I'm moving really fast. Dr. Tatum says, "Active racist behavior is equivalent to walking fast on the conveyor belt. Passive racist behavior is equivalent to standing still on the walkway. No overt effort is being made, but the conveyor belt moves the bystander along to the same destination as those who are actively

---

21 https://www.beverlydanieltatum.com/published-works/

walking."[22] I love that analogy. I think it is a very powerful illustration of passive racism.

The theme in this chapter is the role of pastors, ministers, apostles, prophets, evangelists, and teachers as it relates to the dismantling of racism in the Church. Ministers of the Gospel are called to preach. What is the significance of preaching against racism? Romans 1:16, says, "For I am not ashamed of the gospel of Christ: for it is the power of God unto salvation to everyone that believeth..." (KJV). Notice the Apostle Paul says that he is **not ashamed** of the Gospel!

ASK YOURSELF . . .

•   *Am I ashamed of the Gospel of Christ?*

The Gospel of Christ is the power of God unto salvation. That word *salvation* means deliverance, wholeness, healing, restoration, and provision. It means to be saved. Paul says that the Gospel is God's power to salvation to everyone that believes. This is significant because racism is a generational curse. Racism is a demonic spirit of division. In fact, racism is a mental stronghold that requires spiritual weaponry to eradicate.

General teaching on love, generosity, and service is wonderful. We all teach on love, we all teach on generosity, and we all teach on service, but general teaching alone will not break the power of spiritual forces. General teaching will not break the power of this way of thinking because racism is a mindset that has been established over time.

Jesus once dealt with a man that was possessed of a demon in Mark 5, and He asked the demon, "What is your name?" Jesus understood the importance of addressing those spirits. Some spirits must be directly addressed. We can't sidestep them; we have to confront them.

Racism is a generational curse and an evil spirit which has to be

---

22 https://www.beverlydanieltatum.com/published-works/

broken. It is a way of thinking established over time, fortified by cus-
tom, and resistant to change. The only thing that will break the power
of a deep generational stronghold like racism over the Church is the
preaching of the Gospel. You already know that if people are going to
get saved and know the truth, we must preach the truth.

The Apostle Paul, under the inspiration of the Holy Spirit, said,
"For whosoever shall call upon the name of the Lord shall be saved.
How then shall they call on him in whom they have not believed? and
how shall they believe in him of whom they have not heard? and how
shall they hear without a preacher? So then faith cometh by hearing..."
(Romans 10:13-14, 17 KJV). Faith for deliverance from sin and addic-
tive habits comes by hearing. Faith for healing comes by hearing. Faith
for spiritual maturity comes by hearing. Therefore, Christians will not
be delivered from racism without hearing.

The principle of scripture is that different kinds of seeds produce
different kinds of crops. Mark 4:26 says, "So is the kingdom of God, as
if a man should *(or must)* cast seed into the ground" (KJV). Galatians 6:7
says, "whatsoever a man soweth, that shall he also reap" (KJV).

**It is an unrealistic expectation that racism will be broken
over the Body of Christ without sowing Gospel seeds.**

It is an unrealistic expectation to think our members will be delivered without hearing the truth of the Gospel. We must sow this seed
about race, racism, and racial equality. Black pastor and minister, you
must preach and teach clear, specific, biblical lessons on race, racism a
racial reconciliation. Why? Your anointed teaching will aid and guide
your members in properly processing their emotions in a constructive
way. Your members have some emotions about race and not all of those

emotions about racism are constructive or wholesome. So, you must preach and aid them in processing their emotions about race in a proper and constructive way.

For example, the Bible warns us in Ephesians 4:26 that we are to be angry and sin not. It is our role to teach our congregations about race, racism, and racial reconciliation so they will be able to constructively process their emotions and obey Ephesians 4:26. Our preaching will break the power of reactionary racism that may be over our congregations. I am sure we all have members in the Church who are struggling with reactionary racism and need to be delivered. Another emotion our preaching will destroy is the stronghold of inferiority. I know that when you have had a black point of reference, a black experience, and a black world view in a majority white environment, then you are likely to have some issues and a sense of inferiority because our environment constantly tells us that we are inferior. The only thing that will break the stronghold of inferiority over our members is preaching the Gospel. They need to know who they are in Christ.

There is some debate about whether or not black people or black Christians can be a racist. Some say black people cannot be a racist because they do not have institutional control. In other words, black people don't control the major institutions in America. Black people don't have authority control. They don't make the laws, policies, practices, and they don't create the norms that other races live by. For that reason, some say that a black person or a black Christian cannot be a racist. Whether you believe or agree with that or not, one thing is certain. There is no doubt that there are black Christians in the Church that are prejudiced and struggle with hate and discrimination.

I was talking to one of the most wonderful, amazing, gifted, godly leaders that we have in our Church. He told me about a season in his life before he got saved that he hated white people. He said that what I have been preaching and teaching is true. He said he knew what I am teaching is necessary. He looked me in the face and said, "I know any person who wants to, can be delivered from hating white people because God saved me, filled me with the Spirit, and delivered me from that hatred in my heart." Then he said, "Pastor, you know the funny thing? After I got saved, I ended up in a predominantly white Church with a white pastor. You know, God does have a sense of humor."

Years ago, the Spirit of God began to deal with me about racism and said a couple of things specifically to me. He said, "Do not be prejudiced." Usually, when God tells you not to do something, it is because you are doing it. Then He said, "Racism needs to be dealt with." I began to teach years ago on racism in the Church, and race, racism, and racial reconciliation years ago. I am sharing something with you that is important to you because as black people, we tend to think that only white people need to hear the Word about this. We need to hear the Word, too.

I want to address the white pastor, minister, apostle, prophet, evangelist, and teacher. You must preach and teach clear, and specific biblical lessons on race, racism, and racial reconciliation. I was talking to another church member who at one point was under a white pastor. She said that her white pastor did not feel comfortable teaching or preaching on race.

There are many white pastors who feel uncomfortable teaching on race, racism, and racial reconciliation; nonetheless white pastors are called to preach and motivate their white members to be open and participate in honest, transparent discussions on race and racism without defensiveness. If white ministers don't, their members will not be able to talk about it. It is no different than preaching on evangelism.

If pastors don't preach and teach them on evangelism and how to win people to Christ, they will not feel comfortable because they won't have the knowledge base. They are going to have to have faith to be transparent and talk to others of different races without defensiveness.

Pastors, you have members in your church who are involved with, operate in, and participate in generational racism. You have people in your church that need deliverance. Your godly teaching empowered by the Holy Spirit will destroy the stronghold of superiority and send the demonic spirit of racism back to hell. It is impossible for you as a white Christian to not deal with the sense of superiority because you have a white frame of reference, a white worldview, a white experience, and you live and navigate in a predominantly white-led America. It is impossible that you at some point have not or will not struggle with the sense of superiority.

You may be the most wonderful pastor on the planet earth. Maybe you were brought up by Christian parents, maybe you even had black family members and friends and say you do not have prejudice in your heart. However, you cannot say that for all your members. Therefore, you've got to preach to them.

I have been teaching this on television for years and a white pastor invited me to speak at his church. I was all excited and told the congregation, "I'm going to be preaching over here I'd like for you to go with me." I'm thinking that we would experience some racial reconciliation happening there. I felt it would be a great and significant time together. I thought, "We are going to get together and mingle and all that and I'm going to preach and we're going to connect."

We went to the church and a large number of our members went to the predominantly white church with me. When we got to the church, there were very few white members who came; most of their members stayed away. Those who came all sat in the back. Here I am preaching a sermon. All my members sat up in the front and the few white members who came sat in the back. The pastor and I didn't talk about it. I don't know whether he was embarrassed or what, but I did my best. It was like me preaching to my own congregation.

If you don't preach, you are going to have a church full of people who have racism on the inside of them because faith comes by hearing God's Word.

ASK YOURSELF . . .

- *Would you be able to push aside any uneasiness you may feel, to teach on race, racial reconciliation, or racism? Yes or No? Why or Why not?*

CHRISTIANITY AS A BRAND IS NOT THE ANSWER

The Kellogg company is a cereal brand. Under the Kellogg brand, there are different cereals. There is Froot Loops, Frosted Flakes, Raisin Bran, and Rice Krispies. All these are cereals of the Kellogg brand. It is unfortunate that in the Church in America, we have Christianity as a brand. Branded Christianity causes Christians to fall from having a voice to becoming a vote. God did not create the Church to be a vote. God gave the Church a voice. We are supposed to be a voice to this world, but because we have embraced a branded form of Christianity, we have fallen from being a voice to being a vote.

People, and even politicians, don't want to hear our voice. They just want our vote. That is what we are. We are a vote. Branded Christianity embraces some parts of the Bible and excludes or edits other parts of the Bible, kind of like the slave Bible.

Branded Christianity is a politicized version of Christianity.

Believers can register under any party affiliation that they choose or are led to connect with, and they can even be and should be active in politics. However, they should not identify Christianity or the Church with a political party. Identifying the Church and Christianity with a party is inherently divisive. I am challenging the Church to speak out, but we've got to get to the point where we are not politicizing Christianity. We must declare the unadulterated truth rooted both in God's written and Living Word.

Many white evangelical ministers and leaders believe and communicate that the Republican party is the party for committed Christians. The Republican party leans more toward the Biblical view of right-to-life of the unborn and heterosexual marriage. They highlight the party's platform and position on abortion, same sex marriage, conservative values, and how their position lines up with Scripture. However, the Republicans and many White evangelical ministers are silent on the issues of racism and racial equality. A muted voice. James 2:9 says, "If you show partiality, you commit sin, and are convicted by the law as transgressors."

If you want to know how God feels about racism, read Numbers 12:1-10. It says Miriam and Aaron spoke against Moses because of the Ethiopian woman he had married. They just hated the fact that he married a black woman. Read all of Numbers 12:1-10 but focus on verses 9 and 10 and see how God responded.

So the anger of the LORD was aroused against them, and He departed. And when the cloud departed from above the tabernacle, suddenly Miriam became leprous, as white as snow. Then Aaron turned toward Miriam, and there she was, a leper. (Numbers 12:9-10)

Racism is a sin, yet many in the Republican party and many white evangelicals believe there is no systemic racism, there is no white privilege, that racial discrimination was resolved in the '60s with the Civil Rights movement, and is evidenced by the two-term presidency of President Barack Obama. The subtle message of the Republican party and many white evangelical ministers is that if black people would stop being lazy, work hard, and stop being bad, they could get ahead.

When we look at the Democratic party's platform and position, we see words like social justice, racial equality, and equal opportunity. Those things connect to Galatians 3:28, "There is neither Jew nor Greek, there is neither slave nor free, there is neither male nor female;

for you are all one in Christ Jesus." The Democratic party leans more toward the biblical command to lift the poor and defend the rights of the oppressed. Jeremiah 22:16 says, "'He gave justice and help to the poor and needy, and everything went well with him. Isn't that what it means to know me?' says the Lord" (NLT). Many Republicans believe too much aid to the poor is socialism.

We need to look at the whole Bible to understand God's attitude toward these issues. Acts 10:34-35 says, "God is no respecter of persons but in every nation, ethnos, race of men, those who fear him and work righteousness are accepted of God" (KJV). In other words, racism is a sin. In Luke 10:30-37, in the parable of the good Samaritan, Jesus taught about a man who risked his life and gave materially to help someone of a different race and a different religion.

However, during the Jim Crow era, over four thousand people were lynched for no other reason than they were black. That's not all the people that have been killed through our history by racism. Racism not only kills people, it kills accomplishment, motivation, potential, aspiration, and if you want to really sum it up, it kills unity.

**Racism is the number one thing standing
between America and the Church having revival.**

You can fast and you can pray and advocate banning of any one of a number of social issues, but we are not going to have revival in America until we start preaching and talking about racism. God's got some great churches doing some great things, but America will not have revival until racism is broken over the Church.

ASK YOURSELF . . .

- Is the American Church a voice or a vote?

Have we fallen from being a voice to becoming a vote? Everybody wants our vote. Jesus is not a Republican, Jesus is not a Democrat, and Jesus is not an Independent. No party or candidate is right on all issues and beliefs that Christians value. You cannot put one party up and say this is the Christian party because you would not be telling the whole truth. No party embraces everything that the Bible is talking about. The Gospel should not be tied to a party, a candidate, or a politician. In Christ, there is neither conservative nor liberal and there is neither right nor left. The Bible says that we are one in Christ. Christ's Church should be above all these parties.

We should be a voice to these parties, not just a vote.

Branded Christianity leads to selective mutism. Selective mutism is a severe anxiety disorder that prevents people from speaking in certain social situations and not speaking in other settings or situations. When you have selective mutism, then you may be in one environment and you can really talk, and you go to another environment and feel you can't say anything. That's what we have when we make the Church political. We end up with selective mutism and it becomes the reason we see things we know are not right about candidates, but we won't say anything because we've turned Christianity into a party. 2 Corinthians 4:3-4 says, "But if our gospel be hid, it is hid to them that are lost in whom the god of this world has blinded the minds of them that believe not lest the light of the glorious gospel of Christ who is the image of God should shine unto them" (KJV).

**The only thing that is going to bring people
out of the darkness of racism is the Gospel. Repentance of racism
must be preached in an uncompromised way.**

REFLECTION STEPS

Begin by reviewing the scriptures presented in this chapter. Record your insights.

Romans 10:13-14, 17
Mark 4:26
Galatians 6:7
Ephesians 4:26
Numbers 12:1-10
Galatians 3:28
Jeremiah 22:16
Acts 10:34-35
2 Corinthians 4:3-4

Then review these Power Points set apart in Chapter 5.

*It is an unrealistic expectation that racism will be broken
over the Body of Christ without sowing Gospel seeds.*

*Racism is the number one thing standing between America and the
Church having revival.*

*The only thing that is going to bring people
out of the darkness of racism is the Gospel.
Repentance of racism must be preached in an uncompromised way.*

Dare to Confront with the Truth and Act Justly

As you read through these Power Points, what did God "dare" you to do to begin to "unmute" the members of the Body of Christ that may be living under the wrong historical information.

_____

_____

_____

_____

_____

_____

Pray and ask God to show you the first steps He wants you to take with each of the people you have listed. Perhaps use some of the questions asked in this chapter.

- Am I ashamed of the Gospel of Christ?
- Is the American Church a voice or a vote?

Record in a journal the response you received. Continue praying for revelation for each of these people.

Chapter 6
Why Some White People Struggle Talking about Racism

Conversations on race and racism are difficult, but necessary. Robin DiAngelo is a white anti-racist educator and lecturer. In her book, "White Fragility," she both asks and answers the question, "Why is it hard for white people to talk about racism?" She discusses in a clear, compassionate, and honest way the emotional responses such as anger, fear, and guilt, along with defensive behaviors such as argumentation, silence, and withdrawal white people have when they experience racial stress and discomfort. She said in her opening statements that she was mainly writing to a white audience and using her insider status to challenge racism. What she meant by insider status is this is a white person talking to white people and challenging them about racism. [23]

On the other hand, I want to discuss this subject from both an outsider's status and prayerfully a spiritual perspective. First, I want to say that I am not talking about whether white people are racist or

---

23 www.goodreads.com/work/quotes/58159636

not. I personally don't believe all white people are racists or that every white person struggles talking about racism. I personally know whites who are open, secure, and transparent in their discussions about race and their willingness to connect. However, I want to talk about three roadblocks to open and transparent communication: blindness or blind spots, lack of empathy, and denial.

Blindness or a Blind Spot. A blind spot is a roadblock to white people opening up freely and talking about racism. Matthew 7:5 says, "First cast out the beam (the wood or log) out of thine own eye, then shall thou see clearly to cast out the mote (the speck or the dust) out of thy brother's eye" (KJV). In this particular text, Jesus says that there is something in our own eye that keeps us from seeing clearly. Now, racism is very apparent to many people of color. We see it very clearly and other minorities who may be victimized by racism see it very clearly, but it is a blind spot to many white people. Remember, I'm not talking to white people in general, I'm talking to Christians. I am speaking to the Church.

What is a blind spot?
- A blind spot is a gap in a person's perception that blinds them from seeing the truth about themselves and others.
- A blind spot is a complete lack of insight about how one's behavior is affecting others.
- A blind spot causes a refusal to listen and affects us in a negative way.
- It produces defensiveness, anger, and justification that will shut down the conversation.

Since everyone has blind spots, we all need someone to tell us the truth, even at the expense of hurting our feelings. Natalie Grant, a white award-winning singer and her husband composer, Bernie Herms, revealed recently that they lost thousands of followers after speaking out against racism after the death of George Floyd.

I read a post by someone who spoke of their discontent with them speaking out against racism. See whether you can see a blind spot. Grant's husband posted on Instagram some of the criticism and abuse they had received, "You should just shut up...," "Stick to what you're best at," "Just keep writing and singing your songs," "You're not helping," "You're just another out of touch liberal celebrity creating more division". We have a white Christian couple speaking out against racism and then we have this post from someone that I take was white. This person did not see the connection between Natalie Grant and her husband's Christianity and speaking out against racism. I consider that a blind spot. It is a gap in the person's perception.

So, what is it going to take to remove those blind spots? I think it is going to take prayer. As Christians, we are going to have to always be asking God to search us, evaluate us, and give us feedback because we don't always see ourselves. I also think it is going to take more than just us praying. I think we are going to have to have godly, honest feedback. We must be willing to listen and believe that there is a blind spot in this area.

A Lack of Empathy. Empathy is the ability to relate to the thoughts, emotions, and experiences of others. There is something about when people show that they understand, you end up getting closer to that person but when people are indifferent, it just continues to drive a wedge there. There are three distinct kinds of empath: emotional empathy, cognitive empathy, and emphatic empathy or emphatic concern.

Emotional empathy is the ability to feel what someone else feels.

Cognitive empathy is the ability to understand another person's perspective.

Emphatic concern is the ability to sense what another person needs from you.

Empathy is scriptural.
"Be happy with those who are happy, and weep
with those who weep."
(Romans 12:15 NLT)

I want to give you an example of what empathy looks like on a racial level. First, let's look at what empathy does **not** look like. We are in a relay race where one person runs, hands the baton to another runner, and so on until they cross the finish line. I've got the baton in my hand at the starting gate and I represent the black race. You have the baton in your hand, and you represent the white race. The horn sounds and as a white person with the baton, you're going to hand that baton to your next generation, and every different generation is going to hand that baton on to the next.

However, when I take off running in my lane, I have weights on me. I have the weight of the black skin weighing me down, but you are running unhindered. I have 246 years of slavery that's weighing me down, but you are still running freely in your lane. Then, I have black codes and violence, and the weight of the Jim Crow era and segregation, but you are just running and handing that baton to the next generation. I've got discriminatory legislation, Gerrymandering, and voter suppression weighing me down.

We look up to the generation we are currently in, you have received the baton and you are at the 80-yard line, but I'm at the 20-yard line. You turn around and look at me and tell me that the playing field is level and if I would just work hard, not be lazy, and not be bad that I could be where you are. When we started the race, you had no weights and I had all these weights on me, but you don't understand why things are unfair.

When you tell me that there is no systemic racism and that the playing field is level, to me that is **a lack of empathy**. It tells me that you don't realize that the gap in wealth that you have as a white person in America and the authority that whites hold. We all know there is a gap between blacks and whites when it comes to wealth, position, and authority, but what you don't fully understand is the **only** reason there is a gap is because of **unfair competition**.

A person who is running in their lane with no weights against a person running in their lane and they've got all these weights, the only reason you are ahead of me is because of unfair competition. I believe that when white people will just be honest and see that the game was rigged and wasn't fair in the beginning, it will release empathy.

**When empathy is created in the heart of a person
then it will lead to compassion, not sympathy.**

There is something about compassion that motivates people to action. Sympathy or pity simply says, "I feel so sorry for you," but compassion is different. In Matthew 14:14, it says that when Jesus saw the multitude, He was moved with compassion and He healed their sick. You see, compassion moves you to act and to help, to give aid, and to give support.

I was watching the protests on television and a black protester was peacefully kneeling several yards away from and facing a line of police in full protective gear. A white protestor came up, knelt right in front of the black protestor facing the police officers. Later, a reporter asked the white protestor, "Were you afraid when you were kneeling in front of the black protestor," the white protestor answered *no*. When the reporter asked why he wasn't afraid, the white protestor said, "Because I am white."

The white protestor demonstrated empathy. The ability to feel what someone else feels. The black protestor probably felt some sense of fear, inhibitions, apprehension. The white protestor showed courage, which is not the absence of fear; it is doing what is right in spite of what you feel. It is the ability to understand another person's perspective. He understood that it was a big deal to kneel in front of all those police officers there in protective gear and the ability to sense what another person needs from you. The black protestor didn't ask for it, but the white protestor understood what he needed. That is empathy birthed out of humility. Jesus said it this way, "Blessed are the meek."

A Christian who has the nature of Jesus on the inside of them, but who does not feel any compassion nor any empathy toward racial equality, none whatsoever, seems very off base to me.

Denial. Denial is a refusal to believe or accept something as true. It is a refusal to believe. There are many white Christians who are in denial when it comes to systemic racism. Revelation 3:17-18 says, "You claim to be rich and successful and to have everything you need. But you don't know how bad off you are. You are pitiful, poor, blind, and naked. Buy medicine for your eyes, so that you will be able to see" (CEV). I was listening to a white Christian who was very adamant and very dogmatic declaring there is no systemic racism. I believe that the root of denial is that white people view life from a white point of reference, a white world view, and white experience.

It is easy to be in denial when you don't have a point of reference. In other words, if you have a white point of reference, white world view, and white experience, you must somehow project yourself. You need to listen to someone who has a different point of reference, a different world view, and a different experience. I believe that white people make the mistake of believing that their experience is black people's experience as well. It is denial of systemic racism.

I also believe that there is a denial of white privilege. Now, this designation and term "white privilege" disturbs white people.

- White privilege does **not** suggest that all white people are wealthy and have never struggled in life or that life was easy growing up.

- White privilege does **not** assume that everything a white person has accomplished is unearned because many white people have worked very hard and made many sacrifices to achieve their level of success.
- White privilege does **not** mean that a white person is a racist.
- We are **not** saying white people have cheated to obtain what they possess.

Cory Collins says, "White privilege is a legacy." [24] Historically, being white was a requirement to be a citizen of the United States. White status and citizenship brought certain advantages. On the other hand, being black brought certain disadvantages.

Frances E. Kendall says, "White privilege is having greater access to power and resources than people of color in the same situation." [25] White privilege is a built-in advantage separate from the level of income, separate from effort, and separate from talent.

Allow me to give you some illustrations.

- White privilege is the ability to move through your professional and personal world without even thinking about race. In other words, white people have challenges, adversity, difficulties, and problems. We have the same challenges, adversity, difficulties, and problems, but we also have challenges just with our skin color. We have stuff plus stuff. The only time white people really think about their skin color and race is when they go into a predominantly black space, like they visit a black church. All of a sudden, they sense and think about race. White privilege means their skin color doesn't make their life more challenging.

---

24 https://courageousconversation.com/what-is-white-privilege-really/

25 franceskendall.com

- White privilege is having high representation in life. They see themselves with 64 percent of the population. They see themselves just about everywhere which brings them a comfort level. When they look in a magazine, in a book, or on television, they see themselves. Oftentimes, black people have to find themselves.
- Usually, white people have positive portrayals in the media. When a black person is portrayed in the media, it is reported that they shot, killed, or robbed somebody. The sad thing about the portrayal black people get in the media is that's a small percentage of black people. Most black people are not robbing, stealing, or killing. That's a small percentage, but that is how they are portrayed in the media.
- White privilege is having the benefit of the doubt. It is the presumption of innocence. In other words, whites are innocent until proven guilty and blacks are usually guilty until proven innocent. It is the presumption of innocence that is an advantage.
- Whites are more likely to be believed or trusted. A black person has a product they need to return to the store but have lost the receipt. A white person has a similar situation, but the black person will have more challenges returning an item without a receipt than a white person.

Recently in New York City, a white woman out walking her dog falsely accused a black man who was a bird watcher. The black man was videotaping her while she was talking to him, and it went viral. On the videotape, she said, "I'm going to call the police and tell them that an African American man is attacking me and my dog." Well, in reality, the black man was simply telling her that she needed to have her dog on a leash in that particular area because it was a leash-mandatory area.

She called the police, got really emotional, and said that the black man was attacking her. Later on, everybody knew she was lying, and she did lose her job. She felt that her word would have more weight than an African American man and could get away with lying. That has been true historically.

- Whites are more likely to be treated as individuals than having some group tag placed on them like violent, aggressive, and lazy.
- Whites are less likely to be handled roughly by police officers. They can count on police protection. Historically, we are not sure how we will be handled once we are put into the police car.
- Whites are less likely to be followed around in a store by clerks or security guards.
- Whites are more likely to receive compassion and survive mistakes. A white person can go in prison, come out with a record, and it's easier for the white person to get a job than the black person with the record. A white male with a criminal record will get just as many calls back in response to a job interview as a black male without a criminal record.
- White privilege is having their history as a part of the main curriculum, not being taught as an elective. Often, black history is an elective, if it is taught at all. Many schools don't even teach it. White history is generally a part of the main curriculum.
- White privilege is moving into an area and the neighbors will be neutral or pleasant to them. Black people move into the same neighborhood and it doesn't matter whether they are professional, have great jobs, and are educated, they may have to deal with whites who are not neutral and not pleasant.

I want to share a social media post that I believe summarizes everything that I've talked about from blind spots to lack of empathy to denial. This was posted by a white person on social media.

"I grew up a Chicago Cubs fan. Ernie Banks was one of my favorite players. Ernie Banks was a black baseball player. I never saw him as a black or white guy, and I refuse to do so. This whole race argument is pathetic. A very few tragic events don't define anything. China has to be laughing all the way to the bank in their minds. It proves them right. Western culture is a joke."

Saying this whole race argument is pathetic is a lack of empathy and denial. Saying a very few tragic events shows a blind spot, a lack of empathy, and denial. We are talking about over 350 years of discrimination and he says a few very tragic events doesn't define anything.

The key to empathy is spending time with God.
If you spend time with God, you are going to get His heart.
There is no way that you can spend quality time in prayer
and lack compassion and empathy.

REFLECTION STEPS

Begin by reviewing the scriptures presented in this chapter, specifically the ones listed below. Study them and record your insights.

Matthew 7:5

Matthew 14:14

Revelation 3:17-18

Then review these Power Points set apart in Chapter 6.

Empathy is scriptural.
"When others are happy, be happy with them,
if they are sad, share their sorrows"
(Romans 12:15 NLT).

When empathy is created in the heart of a person
then it will lead to compassion, not sympathy.

The key to empathy is spending time with God.
If you spend time with God, you are going to get His heart.
There is no way that you can spend quality time in prayer and lack com-
passion and empathy.

Dare to Confront with the Truth and Act Justly

As you read through these Power Points, what did God "dare" you to do to begin to "unmute" the members of the Body of Christ. Are there any adjustments that you need to make? What are they? What actions will you take to address them?

_____

_____

_____

Record in a journal the response you received. Continue praying for revelation for each of these people.

Chapter 7
Lessons from a Christian Racist

Our Christian racist is the Apostle Peter. We are going to use his story in Acts and Galatians to talk about roots and remedies of racism in the Church. Roots or the root system of a plant provide water and food to the plant from soil. The root system of the plant also keeps the plant upright and in place.

There are four roots that feed and keep racism in place.
- Pride
- Superiority
- Ignorance
- Fear

We are going to be studying Peter's racism because we see these four roots in his life. In Acts 10:13-16, the Bible tells us, "There came a voice to him. Rise Peter, kill and eat. But Peter said, Not so Lord; for I have never eaten any thing that is common or unclean. And the voice *spake* unto him again the second time, What God hath cleansed *that* call not thou common. This was done thrice . . . " (KJV).

Pride. We see Peter's pride, a primary root of racism. Notice in the text, God said one thing and Peter said another. God said rise, kill, and eat, but Peter said not so. **Pride is when God says one thing and we say another.** Pride keeps people from acknowledging their shortcomings, weaknesses, and sins. Pride keeps people from repenting, from accepting responsibility without justification or excuses.

Pride talks when one should be listening. In chapter 6, I was talking about blind spots and how it is important to have others outside our circle speak into our lives and give us feedback because we can't see ourselves. Pride talks when we should be listening. If we have been the expert on most things and then come to a subject where we don't have the expertise, then it is important for us to listen rather than to talk.

Superiority. The second root that holds racism in place is superiority or a superiority complex. In Acts 10:28, "Peter told them, [referring to Cornelius] you know it is against our law for a Jewish man to enter a Gentile's home like this or associate with you" (NLT). This is after the Holy Spirit instructed Peter to cross over racial lines and to go to Cornelius' home and share the Word. He says this to a group of people that were hungry to learn and grow. It is indicative of the fact that Peter had a superiority complex. Peter believed that he was superior to the Gentiles because of his racial and religious heritage. **Superiority or a superiority complex hinders fellowship, but it also hinders mutual respect.**

Pause for a Moment . . .
- I want you to look straight down and look forward at the same time.
- What did you discover?
- Did you find it is impossible to look straight down and look forward at the same time?

It is impossible to look down on any person, race, or ethnicity and at the same time treat them as an equal. We can't always be looking up and feel equal to others either. If we are always looking up, there is no way we can feel equal to anybody. So, equality simply says that we look at each other. You look at me and I look at you. I'm not looking down and you're not looking down. I'm not looking up and you're not looking up. We are looking at each other.

However, a superiority complex keeps us from viewing others as equals. It requires developing a biblical mind renewal and intentionality for white people to not feel superior to black or other ethnic people in America because white people are a majority race in America. The white population in America is around 64 percent. The black population in America is around 12 to 13 percent and there is a huge wealth gap, position gap, and authority gap between whites and blacks. This is true of other ethnic groups in America as well.

Also, whites usually operate on the giving side. If you are a majority in a society in terms of population and there is a huge wealth gap, position gap, and authority gap, you are usually on the giving side helping blacks and other ethnic groups, not the other way around. White people must be intentional and renew their minds to not think that blacks and other ethnic groups are inferior or look down on them. Such humility is going to require some work. Likewise, it requires a biblical mind renewal and intentionality especially for black people to not feel inferior to whites.

Now when I say intentionality, I believe it goes all the way back to our formative years. There was no doubt in my mind that if my mama had to vote for the smartest person on the planet, she would vote for me. She always talked about how smart I was from a little kid all the way up to college. She always bragged about how smart I was. She created in me a sense of confidence that I could excel on an academic level. Whether it was going from one elementary school to middle school, or to two different high schools, I excelled academically. I was always on the honor roll and always in the honor society. I went to a predominantly black HBCU, college my freshman year, to a military school where there were only two blacks, and then I went to another college where there were maybe 20 percent black. I excelled in every place. It didn't make any difference what environment I was in because my mother was intentional about building me up in that particular area.

Years ago, we built a family activity center at Faith Chapel and it cost twenty-six million dollars. It has six domes that include an indoor playground for kids, a state-of-the-art gym, a twelve-lane bowling alley, and other fun things in the other domes. We call it the Bridge because we wanted to bridge the community. We wanted to be a bridge between the community and us, so it wasn't just built for our members and it wasn't just built for black people. I felt led of the Spirit that it needed to be very excellent. I wanted young black kids to be able to see a high quality in their space, in their environment, so that they could believe for nice things intentionality. I wanted people to walk in that facility and be inspired, intentionality. Whatever we see a lot of, we believe.

Ignorance. The third thing that holds racism in place is ignorance. Acts 10:28 says, "Peter told them, 'You know it is against our laws for a Jewish man to enter a Gentile home like this or to associate with you. **But God has shown me** that I should no longer think of anyone as impure or unclean'" (NLT). In other words, he was saying, I was ignorant but God has given me some more insight and knowledge. Ignorance can be the absence of knowledge. Peter didn't know that the wall dividing the Jew and the Gentile had been broken down through the finished work of Jesus through the cross. Ignorance can also be embracing false knowledge like the so-called curse of Ham. Ignorance leads to stereotypes and generalizations.

Fear. The fourth root of racism is fear. Peter was instructed by the Holy Spirit to cross racial lines and preach the Gospel to the Gentiles. The power of God fell and when he came back to Jerusalem and his

Jewish peers, who were Christians, criticized him, "When he first arrived, he ate with the Gentile believers, who were not circumcised. But afterward, when some friends of James came, Peter wouldn't eat with the Gentiles anymore. He was afraid of criticism from these people who insisted on the necessity of circumcision" (Galatians 2:12 NLT). The Bible says Peter was afraid of criticism.

Fear is a root that holds racism in place. It's our fear of the unknown, of different cultures, of different backgrounds, rejection, criticism, harm, or loss.

- What will my family, friends, and peers think if I cross over and go to a black Church? Will I be safe?
- As a Pastor, will I lose support? Will I lose money? Will I lose members?
- Will I lose my friends, or family?
- Will I lose my position?

How can Peter, a saved, spirit-filled, Apostle be a racist? If you think about it, when we get saved, nothing happens to our minds. We are brand new on the inside, but nothing happened with our minds. When we come into the Kingdom, we have the same mindset and the same way of thinking. Our way of thinking has been shaped by authority figures, by our environment, by repetitious information, by associations, and by our negative and positive experiences.

When we get saved, none of that changes. Our family doesn't change. In some cases, our environment may not change when we get saved. The people we are around usually do not change. We've still got the same family. If we were brought up in a racist environment, whether it's black or white, then getting saved doesn't change it. That's why in Romans 12:2 it says, "Don't copy the behavior and customs of this world, but let God transform you into a new person by changing the way you think. Then you will learn to know God's will for you, which

is good and pleasing and perfect" NLT). If we don't get our minds renewed, then we will look, talk, and act like unsaved people.

How do we overcome? How did Peter get delivered from racism?
What were the keys?

I have six remedies I would like to examine.
- Prayer
- Epiphany
- Obedience to the Holy Spirit
- Acclimation
- Confrontation
- Transparency

Prayer. Acts 10:2 says Cornelius, "He was a devout, God-fearing
man, as was everyone in his household. He gave generously to the poor
and prayed regularly to God" (NLT). It was in prayer that Cornelius
had a vision in which he was instructed by an angel to send for Peter.
It was also in prayer that Peter had a vision and was instructed by the
Holy Spirit to go to Cornelius' house. Cornelius and Peter were both
praying, and both received instructions.

It is important to spend quality time with God in prayer. It will
break those strongholds. It will break that mindset.

**Prayer is a powerful aid to removing blind spots,
creating empathy, and overcoming denial.**

Epiphany. An epiphany is an illuminating discovery. It is a realiza-
tion; a moment of certain great revelation or insight and it changes you.
In Acts 10:28, Peter had an epiphany and said, "But God has shown me

that I should no longer think of anyone as impure or unclean." (NLT). Peter had a revelation of his own racist attitude and feelings of superiority. He said, "God has shown me that I should never call any man common or unclean." Peter didn't know he was a racist. Remember, racism can occur both at an unconscious and conscious level. Racism can be both active and passive.

Obedience to the Holy Spirit. Acts 10:19-21 says, "Meanwhile, as Peter was puzzling over the vision, the Holy Spirit said to him, 'Three men have come looking for you. Get up, go downstairs, and go with them without hesitation. Don't worry, for I have sent them.' So Peter went down and said, 'I'm the man you are looking for. Why have you come?'" (NLT).

The Holy Spirit told Peter not to doubt and to follow the three men He had sent to Peter. Peter obeyed the Holy Spirit and then went back to Jerusalem and was criticized by his Jewish peers, Peter said the Holy Spirit led me.

**If we are going to dismantle racism,
we must obey the Holy Spirit and be both led and empowered
by the Holy Spirit.**

You and I need to stop being led by our flesh, our culture, and our comfort zone, because oftentimes God's leadings will contradict our feelings and opinions and lead us outside of our comfort zone. Anytime you are engaging a person of a different race, remember that person has a different point of reference, a different world view, and a different experience. This will be outside of your comfort zone.

I can't count the times I've been led to do something that I was very, very uncomfortable doing. Even doing this book on dealing with racism in the Church, I have felt a sense of discomfort. When I'm teaching and ministering to my congregation, I'm in my comfort zone, but now I'm moving outside of it. Whenever you move outside of your comfort zone, you will feel discomfort.

Acclimation. Acclimation is when you adjust to a new climate, a new situation, a new culture, or a new environment. Acclimation always involves initial discomfort. We will never dismantle racism if we are in our segregated spaces. In Acts 10:23 and 25, Peter had to move outside his comfort zone and associate with a new culture and into a new environment.

A Church in disunity has no authority to speak to a divided land. When we look at the landscape in America, we see a lot of division along racial lines.

Whether you are a Christian who is from the Black, White, Hispanic, Latino, Asian, American, or any other ethnic background, I want you to think about how you would answer the following questions:

- Is there racism in the multi-ethnic movement?
- Is there racism in what we call diversity in the Church?
- Why are the majority of multi-racial churches led by white pastors?
- Why do most multi-racial local churches become diverse by minorities assimilating into predominantly white churches?
- Do you think this indicates that it's difficult for white Christians to cross over and join predominantly black churches?
- Have you perceived that black Christians feel it is a step up to attend white churches and a step down for white Christians to attend black churches?

In Acts 10, God worked on both sides. He sent an angel to speak to Cornelius and Gentile servants went to where Peter was staying. On the other hand, God gave Peter a vision and Peter went to Cornelius' home. The Bible says in Acts 10:34 God is no respect of person.

ASK YOURSELF . . .

- If the Lord led you to cross over into a black space, would you obey Him?

On a podcast recently, a question was asked, "Why does revival tarry?" It is my belief, based on Psalm 133, John 17, Acts 2:1-4, and Acts 13:1, God connects the anointing, His blessing, His glory, and the Church's witness to others to unity and oneness. I believe that it is the racial division in the Church that is hindering revival. I believe revival is going to come, but I believe that the evidence of revival in America will be when whites start crossing over into multi-cultural, multi-racial churches.

The Azusa Street revival began in the spring of 1906 in Los Angeles during the Jim Crow law era. Segregation was basically the law of the land and God caused a revival to hit and that gave birth to modern-day Pentecostalism. That revival in Los Angeles was led by an African American minister named William Seymour. He was the son of freed slaves. It was a multi-racial, supernatural outpouring of the Holy Spirit. In fact, someone said this, the color line was washed away in the Blood of Jesus. It was a model of interracial harmony.

People from all over the world came to the Azusa Street revival, black, white, Latino, Asians, young and old, female, male for this outpouring of the Spirit of God. Signs, wonders, people got saved, people got filled with the Spirit, people were healed, and people were transformed. It lasted for three years, with three services a day, seven days a week. It was a genuine outpouring of the Spirit where the color line was destroyed.

I am convinced beyond a shadow of a doubt that God is going to do something very special through African Americans. It is going to be a supernatural work and the color line will once again be washed away in the Blood of Jesus. There is going to be an outpouring of God's Spirit where folk are not going to think in black, white, red, yellow or brown. They are not going to be thinking male or female. I believe that racial division is blocking it now but it is going to be dealt with. When you begin to see whites crossing over into black spaces you will know that it is beginning.

Confrontation. Confrontation means to come face to face with, to deal with hypocrisy, differences, conflict, compromise, and silence. It means to hold others accountable. When Peter acted in a racially insensitive, prejudicial way toward Gentiles, the Apostle Paul confronted him and pointed out his hypocrisy. That's after Peter had the vision and was led to Cornelius' house. When Peter still yielded to some fear that was connected to racism and separated himself, Paul confronted him.

**It will take confrontation for us not only to have
this move of God to dismantle racism,
but it's going to also take confrontation to maintain it.**

Transparency. The reason we have not dealt with racism is because we have struggled talking about the hard issues. We struggle being transparent. We cannot have revival or a move of the Spirit if we do not talk about the hard things like those issues which have been presented in this book.

REFLECTION STEPS

Begin by reviewing the scriptures presented in this chapter, specifically the ones listed below. Study them and record your insights.

Acts 10:13-16	Acts 10:23 and 25
Acts 10:28	Psalm 133
Galatians 2:11-12	John 17
Romans 12:2	Acts 2:1-4
Acts 10:2	Acts 13:1
Acts 10:19-21	

Then review these Power Points set apart in Chapter 7.

Prayer is a powerful aid to removing blind spots,
creating empathy, and overcoming denial.

If we are going to dismantle racism,
we must be led by and obey the Holy Spirit.

It is going to take confrontation for us not only
to have this move of God to dismantle racism,
but it's going to also take confrontation to maintain it.

Dare to Confront with the Truth and Act Justly

As you read through these Power Points, what did God "dare" you to do to begin to "unmute" the members of the Body of Christ and bring unity and help usher in revival.

_____

_____

_____

Record in a journal the response you received. Continue praying for revelation for each of these people.

Final Word
What Is It Going to Take?

It is going to take mind renewal. Romans 12:2 says, "Be not conformed to this world but be transformed by the renewing of your mind that you may prove, demonstrate, discern the perfect will of God." We exchange our thoughts and our feelings for God's thoughts. However, mind renewal is a process.

We must renew our minds to in Christ realities about who we are, where we are, what we have, and what we can do in Christ. We are going to have to renew our mind to the roles of black people in the Bible, in world history, in American history. We need to pray and get black history in our schools as part of the curriculum. It's going to take us getting in the Word and allowing the Word to lord it over our minds.

I believe beyond a shadow of a doubt that racism will be broken over America. I'm praying for it consistently and I have no doubt that it shall be dealt with by God. As I pray, I take authority over every spirit, every principality, every power, every ruler of the darkness, and all spiritual wickedness in heavenly places. I bind those spirits that would hinder God's perfect plan for His Church. Will you join me in praying for the perfect plan of God to manifest in our churches?

I would encourage you to go back and reread these chapters and then share what you are learning with your friends. I believe God will do something special.

As long as the Church is quiet, we will have no voice in the land. God says, **"A Muted Voice is No Voice."** Let's unmute our voice and have open, honest, relevant, and transformative conversations to dismantle racism (and its offspring of prejudice, hate, and discrimination) today!

About the Author

Mike Moore is the founder and president of Mike Moore Ministries and author of numerous books including the popular *"Weep Not: Overcoming Grief, Disappointment, and Loss"* and *"Moving from Tragedy to Triumph."* He built this global ministry decades ago upon the simple yet profound truth that "The Word of God is the Answer" for every situation. His easy-to-follow messages provide practical ways to apply God's Word to every day, real life circumstances.

He is the Senior Pastor of Faith Chapel. In addition to providing spiritual mentorship to an alliance of pastors, Moore can be seen on his **Answers That Work** television broadcast, YouTube channel, **How To Win** podcast, and at conferences.

He is married to Kennetha and they have two adult children, Michael K. and Tiffany.

About Mike Moore Ministries

Mike Moore Ministries was built upon the simple yet profound truth that "The Word of God is the Answer" to all of life's questions. Through various mediums which include television, digital, and print, Mike Moore teaches that God wants His people to live a prosperous life that encompasses spiritual prosperity, physical health, relationships, mental health, and financial independence.

Additional resources from Mike Moore can be obtained by visiting: **MikeMooreMinistries.org** or by calling toll free **1-866-930-WORD (9673).**

ALSO AVAILABLE

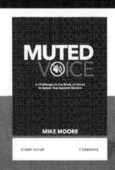

SMALL GROUP GUIDE
ISBN: 978-1-7333716-4-3

STUDY GUIDE
ISBN: 978-1-7333716-3-6

Have open and honest conversations with others in a **small group** setting, whether it is a small group, Bible study, or classroom, that will ultimately lead you to recognize racism and to speak out against it.

The Muted Voice **Study Guide** will provide you with stimulating learning through thought-provoking questions, assist you with mind renewal, and cause introspection through self-reflection. UNMUTE YOUR VOICE TODAY!

available at

amazon

and whereever books are sold

YOU CAN ALSO VISIT **WWW.MUTEDVOICE.INFO** TO MAKE PURCHASES OR TO ACCESS **FREE** CONVERSATION STARTERS (FOR INDIVIDUALS & FOR FAMILIES) AND TO WATCH THE FULL 7-EPISODE DOCUSERIES.